Living in
NORMANDY

Text by Serge Gleizes   **Photographs by Christian Sarramon**
Foreword by Philippe Delerm

Flammarion

CONTENTS

Page 1: A field of flax in the pays de Caux.
Pages 2–3: A view of Etretat.
Left: A manor house in the Le Perche region.

The charm of Normandy

PHILIPPE DELERM

Above: The window in Marine and Philippe Delerme's kitchen. A venerable old quince tree casts its shade over the garden. Facing page: Every spring, the gnarled old apple trees disappear beneath an avalanche of delicate blossoms.

Many of the great tourist regions of France and elsewhere draw the crowds thanks to the sheer drama of their landscapes. Think of the sweeping grandeur of the Alps, the power of the Grand Canyon, the majesty of Ayers Rock standing in solitude in the heart of the Australian outback. Were we to imagine the musical accompaniment to these landscapes, it would have to be a grand orchestral score with plenty of violins, percussion, and clashing cymbals that build to an awesome climax. The landscape of Normandy, on the other hand, brings to mind a gentle piano sonata. The fields and woodlands that stretch from Alençon to Cabourg and from Granville to Giverny are an endless source of quiet harmony and serenity.

As I sat down to try and sum up the essence of the region I call home, an image sprang to mind: a laughing, sunlit stream in a flower-strewn meadow. The grass is lush and green. The stream meanders gently across the field, not because the contours of the land force it to, but simply because it is in no hurry to reach the sea. The rivers of Normandy flow gently through fertile pastureland, their calm waters reflecting overhanging boughs laden with fruit. Driving along the road that follows the sinuous coastline of the Channel between Trouville and Honfleur, I always admire how the opulent green of the meadows and orchards melds harmoniously with the gray and blue of the sparkling waves. Here, in the Pays d'Auge—the geographical heart of Normandy—the grass grows tall and lush. This is the *département* of Calvados—picture-postcard Normandy, where fat cattle roaming free in emerald-green fields provide the rich, creamy milk for the superb cheeses for which the region is famed.

But this is only part of the picture. Normandy also has its wild, untamed corners. Movie directors such as Polanski and Truffaut have re-created the windswept heaths of England and Ireland in the far reaches of the Cotentin. The lofty heights of La Varende in the distance blend into the blue haze of the Pays d'Ouche. The shrouds of mist that veil the forests and the lakes of the Orne *département* and the melancholy solitude of the beaches lying along the northern coast toward Tréport create an ambience very different from that of the sunny meadows and cheerful market towns.

Normandy is a land of contrasts, where driving past lonely fields and copses you turn a corner and suddenly find yourself in a bustling fishing port. Honfleur is one such port; an absolute jewel, with its tall, narrow slate-roofed houses and its colorful fishing smacks lined up at the quayside. Nestled at the foot of a green circle of hills, it is a truly delightful spot. Normandy is rich with such gems. There is the medieval heart of Rouen, miraculously

*Left: Norman gardens
are often just
as charming as
traditional English
gardens, with an
added touch of
elegance and
sensuality.
Right: Apple blossoms.*

preserved almost intact despite being severely bombed during the war, and the majestic curving reaches of the Seine after Jumièges, renowned for its succulent cherries. And the monastery of Bec-Hellouin, where the monks in their simple white robes can often be seen strolling in the dappled woodlands dotted with clusters of hyacinth, or the evanescent beauty of the fields of flax, where the wind creates shimmering ripples of white and blue.

The people of Normandy live in homes as modest and unpretentious as they are themselves—long, low farms protected behind stout walls, ancient half-timbered houses, and buildings built from bricks mellowed by the sun. Normandy reminds me of a fine old lady dressed in pink-and-white finery remembering the dances of her youth, or a fragile blossom on the gnarled branches of a venerable old apple tree. Every spring, the crooked branches of the old apple trees in the orchards disappear under an avalanche of snowy white blossoms, as cheerful as a peal of laughter. The flowers huddle on the branches like gaggles of schoolgirls sharing a secret. Each bloom—five petals of almost transparent white tinged with delicate pink—shakes off the morning dew and lifts its velvety face to the sun. They remind me of rosy-cheeked country maids dancing a merry round.

A *land of magic*

From the air, it looks as if someone had thrown a patchwork quilt over the land. The checkerboard of fields and pastures is dotted with cows contentedly grazing or dozing in flowery meadows. Screaming seagulls swoop from high cliffs around the charming little fishing ports where the way of life has scarcely changed for centuries. Normandy offers a rich harvest of new tastes and sights—winding rivers under skies that pour milky light over the landscape, fields of flax, and narrow country lanes sheltered by tall hedgerows. The Norman houses tucked away in corners of this serene landscape often seem to have grown from the fields themselves. A home in Normandy might be an elegant manor house with a slate roof and a stone dovecote, a tiny cottage peeking out from under a heavy thatch roof, or a splendid early-twentieth-century villa on the cliffs looking out over the Channel.

Historically, Normandy has always been a very wealthy region, with plentiful resources, both agricultural and cultural. As Gustave Flaubert, himself a native of Normandy, wrote, "Some lands are so beautiful that one wishes to hug them to one's chest." In administrative terms, the Normandy region covers five *départements*: Manche, Calvados, Orne, Eure, and Seine-Maritime. These administrative divisions reflect the varying nature of the Norman landscape, from seaside cliffs to gently rolling hills and shady valleys further inland. And while the French say, with some justification, that it always rains in Normandy, it is nonetheless a region of great charm and magic. The rain is precisely what blesses the land with its lush fertility, creating an atmosphere that is anything but melancholy.

Parts of Normandy bear a great resemblance to the delightful rolling downs of southern England. Maybe that is why so many English families are choosing to settle in the region. However, relations with the neighbors just a few miles north across the English Channel have not always been easy. The last man to launch a successful invasion of England—William the Conqueror—was the Duke of Normandy before he won the title of King of England in a battle in 1066. His reign was a great success and he was often held up as an example to rulers in later centuries. With the support of his beloved wife Matilda, daughter of the Count of Flanders, William built defensive castles along the Normandy coast in Falaise and Cherbourg, developed towns such as Saint-Lô and Carentan, and founded the city of Caen. Histories recount that he built the convent of the Holy Trinity and the monastery of Saint Etienne to guarantee his place in Paradise, although the real reason was probably a more prosaic

Left: The abbey
of Bec-Hellouin in the
département of
Eure. The abbey was
founded in 1034 on
the banks of the Bec in
the Risle valley.
In 1041, two monks,
Lanfranc and
Anselme, made the
abbey a great center
of Christian learning.
It suffered greatly
during the French
Revolution and
it was not until after
World War II that
it once again became
a home for the monks.
Facing page:
Coupesarte Manor in
the pays d'Auge, near
Lisieux. This noble old
farmhouse, ringed
by a moat on three
sides, dates back
to the late fifteenth
century. The building's
half-timbered frame is
reflected in the waters
of the moat; the twin
turrets are a reminder
of the region's feudal
past.

attempt to curry favor with the pope. Despite his invasion of England to claim what he saw as his rightful place on the throne, William was a man of peace. The same cannot be said for some of the other Norman kings—the valorous Richard the Lionhearted, and the great warrior king Henry II, husband of Eleanor of Aquitaine. Normandy is also the legendary birthplace of Sir Lancelot and the cradle of many ancient legends and magical rites. It was the home of Joan of Arc; and of Charlotte Corday, famous for murdering the revolutionary leader Marat in his bath in 1793; and, on a more happy note, Marie Harel, the woman who invented camembert. It inspired the creation of great heroines such as Flaubert's Emma Bovary and Alexandre Dumas's Marie Duplessis, better known as *La Dame aux Camélias*, the heroine of Verdi's immortal opera *La Traviata*.

Despite its unparalleled cultural heritage, Normandy is not a land fixated on its past. This is perhaps not surprising given that much of its recent history is intensely painful. World War II brought devastation to the region; Normandy witnessed the 1944 landings of the Allied Forces along its beaches. The 9,386 white crosses in the American Cemetery in Colleville-sur-Mer, overlooking Omaha Beach, are a constant reminder of the sacrifice made by those brave soldiers. Nearby, the German cemetery of La Cambe reminds us that fathers, husbands, fiancés, sons, were bitterly mourned on both sides. From Grandcamp to Ouistreham, the Calvados coast is an open-air memorial to the folly of man.

Watching the dappled light playing over the waters of a sunlit stream, I can well understand how a handful of artists working in the gardens and fields of Normandy created a movement that was to revolutionize the world of painting, overturning centuries of tradition. The first Impressionists spurned the strict rules of genre painting that proclaimed grand historical themes to be the only ones worthy of attention. Instead, they sought to capture the magic of the fleeting moment, leaving the dry, academic atmosphere of the studio behind in favor of open fields and meadows. They were charmed by the salt tang of the sea air, the crashing waves, the swiftly shifting clouds, the white glimmer of the chalk cliffs, the elegant rock formations, the pale light of dawn. The Impressionists were masters of the art of depicting light in all its various qualities. The photographs on the following pages are a fitting homage both to the freshness of their vision and to the superb countryside that inspired it.

Left: The beach at Etretat with the Aval cliff, Manneporte arch, and rock needle in the distance.
Above: The old port of Honfleur.

Seashores and green fields

The Normandy coast

*Preceding spread: The Petites-Dalles beach.
The Impressionist painters fell under the spell
of the changing light on the Normandy coast,
painting it at all hours. Poets and writers
also found inspiration here.
Above: Fishermen in Yport.
Facing page: Left: The lighthouse of Saint-Valéry-
en-Caux. The village of Saint-Valery-en-Caux
is nestled in a sheltered bay. In the nineteenth
century, it rivaled nearby Fécamp as a seaside
resort. Today, it is a quiet fishing port with
a small marina. Top: A path leading to the sea
in Sainte-Marguerite-sur-Mer. Bottom: The beach
at Saint-Valery-en-Caux.*

In Normandy, each of the four seasons brings its own delightful harvest. In fall, there are crops of rosy-red and crisp green apples and forests full of burnished-copper leaves. Winter is the season of slate-gray skies, where clouds and sea seem to meld on the horizon. March and September bring the equinoxes and the drama of the high tides. The artist Paul Huet, who settled in Honfleur in 1820, was fascinated by these tides, painting them over and over again. And then there is summer, when the meadows are heavy with flowers and life along the coast is sweet.

The part of the coastline known as the Côte fleurie—the flowery coast—is at its finest in summer, when the sun sparkles on lush greenery fed by abundant spring showers. Long, sandy beaches invite a stroll along the coastline to gather shells or wade in the shallows. Sometimes, more than half a mile of beach is exposed at low tide. Further along the coast is the Côte d'Albâtre—the alabaster coast—which draws its name from the superb white cliffs, composed of layers of brown flint and calcareous clay the color of semiprecious marcasite. The seawater, heavy with this chalk sediment, is milky white, as ocean waves wear away at the coastline, eroding it inch by inch, year after year. At the cape of La Hève, as much as six feet of coastline is lost every year. When the weather is fine, standing on the outermost limit of the headland, it is just possible to discern traces of where the coastline once stood—over a mile out to sea.

The steep valleys that sweep inland from these cliff tops are also the work of erosion. A walk along the cliffs is an exhilarating experience, but best avoided if you have a fear of heights. Standing on the edge of the headland, buffeted by the wind, looking out over the limestone rocks and the stone needles carved by the relentless action of the waves, the world seems infinitely large, the ocean boundless. The only sound is the rushing of the wind and the waves crashing on the beach far below.

The Surrealists were enchanted by this unique landscape, where the gray ocean meets the sky, making it one of their favorite themes, both in painting and in writing—André Breton, Louis Aragon, and Jacques Prévert were all inspired to write about the sublime beauty of the Normandy coast. But the finest description of the region is surely that of the great nineteenth-century writer Guy de Maupassant, himself born near Dieppe: "From Dieppe to Le Havre, the coast is one uninterrupted cliff standing some hundred meters tall and as straight as a wall…. Here and there, the great line of white rocks suddenly dips, forming a little narrow valley with steeply sloping sides … which leads down from the fields on the cliff top to

the pebble beach below…. Nature started these valleys, which rainstorms turned into ravines…. Sometimes there is a village huddled in the valley, where the wind blowing off the sea whistles between the narrow walls."

From the nineteenth century until today, people have visited the coast as a way of escaping the stresses and strains of the city, with its noise and hectic pace. The jagged cliffs, meandering streams, and chameleon skies of the Normandy coast are the perfect antidote to the demands of urban life. A generation of Romantic writers and artists perfectly understood this almost two hundred years ago, when a trip to Normandy was less adventurous than a voyage to the Alps, but just as popular. Artists and poets came to breathe the fresh air and walk for miles along the pebble beaches, letting the salty tang of the ocean fill their lungs and blow the troubles from their minds. Many of them found the landscape to be a rich source of inspiration. Flaubert, a native of Rouen, found the countryside a great consolation in times of doubt. Erik Satie, another Norman born and bred, was inspired by the music of the rain to compose his superbly evocative Gymnopédies. Baudelaire found the vistas a cure for his melancholy and fell under the spell of Honfleur, writing, "It has always been one of my most cherished dreams to settle in Honfleur." The fishing port inspired him to write the first lines of his superb "L'invitation au voyage," one of the most famous poems in the French language.

The Normandy coastline is several hundred miles in length, about 186 of which belong to the Manche *département*, which boasts eight marinas, nine lighthouses, and a natural park. The coast is anything but monotonous, varying from pebble beaches to staggeringly high cliffs; from tiny fishing villages to elegant seaside resorts; from windswept fields to warm, sandy coves. The meandering waters of the river Sienne give the region much of its character, flowing gently through shady meadows down to the sea. Sheep wander freely along its banks, feeding on the fragrant herbs and wildflowers: delicate, blue globe thistles, wild rye, timothy grass. Toward the sea, a few simple wooden craft lie crookedly on their sides, waiting for the high tide at the next equinox to taste the waves once more.

Geographically, the Normandy coast covers the region between Tréport to the south and Mont-Saint-Michel to the north. The cliffs stretch as far as the eye can see, standing tall and jagged, torn by the combined action of the wind and the waves into peaks and pillars that seem to have been deliberately sculpted by an invisible hand. From Cap d'Antifer and Étretat, the Tilleul cliffs bear not a single trace of a human presence. They are swept bare by

Above: Three wooden huts on the beach in Sainte-Marguerite-sur-Mer.
Left: The port in Saint-Valery-en-Caux, where the ebb and flow of the tide dictates when the sailing boats and fishing smacks can enter and leave the port.

Above: The Petites Dalles beach.
Facing page: An aerial view of Etretat. The cliffs protect the curving beach from the winds that sweep in off the Atlantic. The town became fashionable in 1852 as sea bathing became popular with the upper classes. Wealthy Parisians built the casino, seaside promenade, and numerous villas. Among the best-known visitors were the artist Eugène Isabey and Queen Isabella II of Spain, who rented the Château des Aygues on the hills to the east of the town.

the wind and the endless mist of fine salt spray, while the seagulls wheel screaming overhead. Further along the coast, a few narrow paths—stairs carved directly into the rock, now worn with the passage of time—wind up hundreds of yards from the shore to the cliff tops. On the sand down below, fishermen once abandoned their old fishing smacks here on the shore. Over the years, thatched roofs have been added to the old boats to protect fishing gear from the wind and the rain. A number of these quaint *caloges* have recently been restored.

In Normandy, the tides beat a natural rhythm that governs life in the fishing ports. And since fishing is such a way of life here, every true Norman feels the ebb and flow of the tides in his blood. In Granville, the difference between high and low tide can be as much as fifty feet. It is truly impressive to watch the waves pounding and frothing on the needle-sharp rocks. Just along the coast, in Chausey, the locals count fifty-three islands at high tide and 365 when the waters recede—one for every day of the year. The hamlet of Blainville attests to just how hard life in these fishing villages must have been: the houses are built of local stone and slate, set low and huddled together against the winter storms. There are no shops or schools, just a few cows, a couple of meager fields, and two or three fishing families scratching a living from harvesting shellfish.

The tides dictate the timetables of ferries and hovercrafts, and when the *bisquines*, as the locals call their traditional fishing vessels, can enter and leave the port. The tides also leave a rich harvest behind on the foreshore for the beachcombers who spend hours picking over the sand flecked with spume to find treasures cast up with the seashells and strands of kelp. The author Patrick Grainville, born in Villerville shortly after World War II, described this coast in loving detail: "This quick-running sea makes me think of the swiftness of time…. The Norman sea is gray water, murky, filled with seaweed, sand, and living ooze…. At low tide, the sea huddles and shivers in the distance, an abstract ribbon; then the metamorphosis takes place…. The great cavalcade thunders across the sands…. Exhilaration and the hub-bub of the world re-awaken."

The Cotentin is home to the huge bay of Escalgrain. The Jobourg headlands, lined with jagged reefs, are among the highest cliffs in Europe, standing over 420 feet (130 meters) tall. Protected from prying eyes by a thick screen of ferns, the cove of Vauville has a charming little botanical garden, and the Biville dunes at the base of the cliff are now a protected nature reserve. At Cap La Hague, in the far north of the region, the cliffs wear a thick cloak of heather and the crystal-clear streams plunge suddenly into deep crevasses. The winds here are gentler, and the rocks less harshly jagged, and the fields are greener and very fertile. Here and there, a church spire rises in the distance, promising human companionship. As you drive inland, you will pass ancient manor houses and châteaux, hewn from the local granite, slumbering in the sun.

At dusk, clouds lit by the dying rays of the sun are burnished a deep bronze, illuminating rocky outcrops that resemble the ruins of some prehistoric city destroyed by a cataclysmic earthquake. These jumbled rock formations date back to the Quaternary period, when the

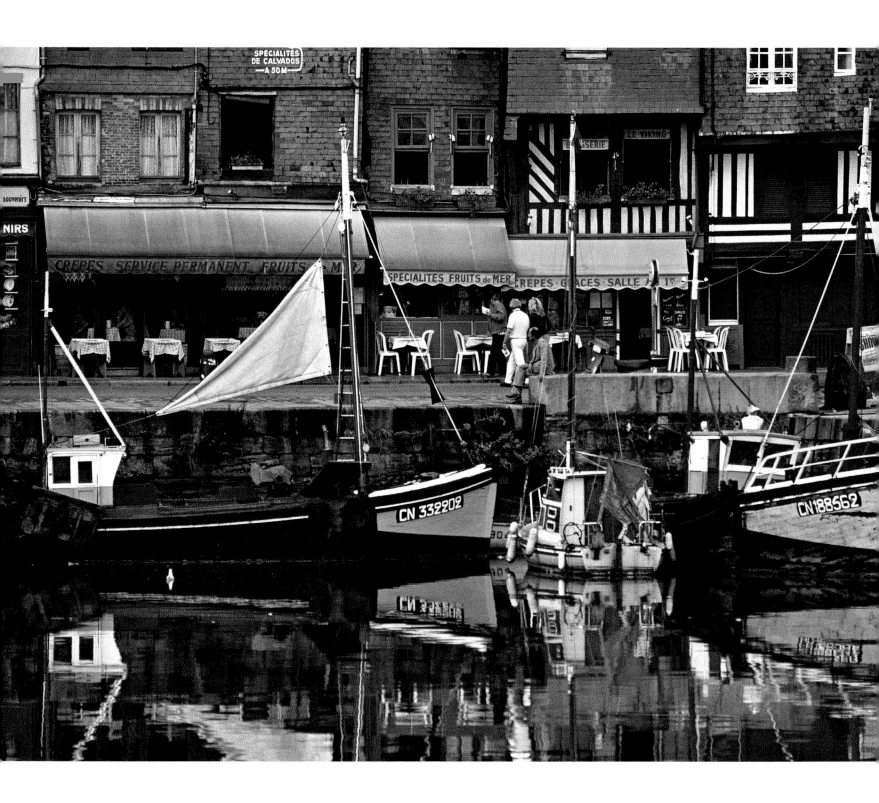

VERT GALANT JOEL KIPS SCULPTEUR FONDEUR

Channel Islands were torn from the mainland and cast into the ocean. The force of wind and waves carved out beaches, coves, and ports. Over millennia, along the Calvados coast, beaches rose and fell; old ports in the pays de Caux are now choked with stones, and the estuary of the Seine has silted up. Towns that were flourishing ports in Roman times are now some way inland. Lillebonne, with its fine Roman amphitheater, is a prime example.

At one end of the Norman coast is the famous Bay of Mont-Saint-Michel, a site of considerable religious importance and the focus of a great historical rivalry, pitting France against England, Catholicism against Calvinism, and Normandy against its neighbor, Brittany. The story behind the monastery of Mont-Saint-Michel is a remarkable one. In the early years of the seventh century, Saint Michael came to Aubert, bishop of Avranches, in three visions. Aubert ordered an oratory to be built to the saint's honor on Mont Tombe, a hill lying just off the coast, thus laying the foundation for one of the great marvels of Christianity. Blocks of granite from Brittany and the islands of Chausey were hoisted over 260 feet (80 meters) up to the summit of the church spire. For a while, the isolated monastery also served as a prison for those convicted of crimes against the government. The place that Victor Hugo called "the great isolated lady of the sands" was placed on UNESCO's list of World Heritage sites in 1979. In the 1960s, a new road was built to the island, replacing a former road that was submerged at high tide.

To the northeast of the Cotentin peninsula, the Saire valley is a delightful spot, where sites of outstanding natural beauty lie side by side with little fishing ports and villages full of old-world charm. One of the best known is Saint-Vaast-la-Hougue, famous for its oyster fisheries, which are just as good as those of its better-known rival, Cancale, in Brittany. Here, from the shore, one can discern the faint outline of the island of Tatihou—the isle of birds—accessible by foot when the tides are at their lowest. The island has an impressive fortress—a reminder of the days when the British posed a real threat to these maritime regions. Barfleur, directly opposite the English coast, is the best-known fishing village in France, famed for its picturesque narrow streets. Climbing up the 233-foot-high (70 m) lighthouse, you have an unparalleled view over the Saint-Marcouf islands, the bay of Veys, and the Grandcamp cliffs. The quayside is lined with rather severe-looking granite houses with piles of lobster pots outside each front door; Barfleur lobster is said to be the best in France. Nearby Port Racine is France's smallest port, but what it lacks in size it more than makes up for in charm, with its fleet of twenty trawlers and the hortensias that brighten up the narrow lanes in summer. Further along the coast, a stroll through the dunes at Pointe d'Agon is an unforgettable experience. Regnéville-sur-Mer, with its ancient houses scattered across the hillside, winding streets, and

Above: The Normandy Bridge, inaugurated in 1995, is one of the highest cable-stayed bridges in the world. Steel cables support a hi-tech frame, much like the pendulum of a grandfather clock. From a distance, the mile-long (two kilometer) bridge looks like a huge sail.
Left: The old port of Honfleur dates back to the seventeenth century.
Following spread: A view of the port in Honfleur and the ships with their azure flags. The slate houses reflected in the waters of the port date from the eighteenth century.

romantic ruined keep, is proud of its heritage as one of the Cotentin's busiest ports. Although the harbor is now silted up, the town thrives on the memory of its past greatness. In the nineteenth century, it had a prosperous lime-burning industry making fertilizer and mortar. As you approach Coutances, the countryside changes; fields become squarer, the sea calmer, the cliffs less steep and less tormented by the wind and spray than those further north.

Deauville, Honfleur, Trouville, Houlgate, Cabourg, Varengeville—these enchanting seaside resorts are strung along the coast like a strand of pearls. They are often very quaint, with a flavor of the nineteenth century about them. Turning the corner of a narrow, shady street, you half expect to see a lady in Edwardian dress shading her ivory skin with a lacy parasol.

Etretat came into fashion thanks to the nineteenth-century novels of Alphonse Karr, once editor in chief of *Le Figaro*. The town is justly famed for its remarkable rock formations; limestone and flint cliffs have eroded into fantastical shapes with evocative names—the hollow needle, the Aval cliffs below the town, the Manneporte arch, and the Amont cliffs above the town, with the church of Notre-Dame-de-la-Garde looking out over the waves. Visiting the town one winter morning, I found it quiet and peaceful, muffled in a shroud of mist. Guy de Maupassant once lived here in a house called La Guillette on the street that now bears his name. He claimed that the town got its name from the sound of pebbles clinking together on the beach (visitors have been forbidden to take pebbles from the beach since 1985). Etretat was also the second home of the composer Jacques Offenbach, who often stayed at the Orphée Manor, which, sadly, burned down in 1861. The elegant spire of the church serves as a reminder of the tragic flight of the Oiseau Blanc, whose pilots failed in their attempt to fly across the Atlantic in 1927. They were last seen over Etretat, and were never heard from again.

Above: Houlgate has many fine examples of traditional Norman seaside architecture. This brick house with a slate roof is typical of the Belle Epoque. Left: Trouville is separated from Deauville by Touques. It is now an elegant beach resort well known for the delightful market held on the quayside every Sunday morning.

Nearby Fécamp is famous for its Benedictine liqueur and the fishing smacks that brave the icy waters off the coast of Newfoundland for codfish. Fewer and fewer of these brave men can earn a living from fishing, turning instead to tourism and other less glamorous yet more lucrative trades such as cod salting and herring pickling.

Deauville is an elegantly old-fashioned resort, where the seafront is lined with luxury boutiques; a discreet reminder of the types of tourists it attracts. Here you can enjoy a horse ride along the beach, or while away a lazy afternoon gazing at the sea under a parasol or in one of the carmine, azure, or orange beach tents. Van Dongen's paintings of Deauville are searing portraits of all the beauty and vacuity of the *beau monde* that vacationed here in bygone years. The casino, the Bar du Soleil, the Pompeii baths, the yacht marina in La Touques are all still as popular as ever with today's fashionable set. The planks of azobe—an African hardwood—that form a path along the one and a quarter miles (two kilometers)

Above: Arromanches and the beaches that witnessed the Allied Landings. The town has a small museum commemorating the events of those historic few days.
Right: The cape of La Hague at the furthest tip of the Cotentin. The cape is dotted with picturesque villages such as Saint-Germain-des-Vaux, Omonville-la-Rogue, and Omonville-la-Petite, where the poet Jacques Prévert spent his last days.

from Deauville to Trouville and Mont Canisy, have lent their name to the local biscuits that every baker in town sells. Deauville is well known internationally thanks to its annual festival of American cinema, as well as other events such as horseracing and the Grand Prix, tennis and golf tournaments, and the world polo championships. In August, racehorse owners flock here from all over the world for the sale of yearlings.

A short walk along the coast takes you to Trouville. There has long been a friendly rivalry between the two resorts, with Trouville claiming to be the more down-to-earth, less precious counterpart to neighboring Deauville. Apart from the beautiful walks and a number of spas specializing in seawater treatments, the superb villas that grace the area are a big attraction. Built in the late nineteenth century by wealthy Parisians seeking refuge from the smoke and noise of the city, elegant homes such as Villa Sidonia, the neo-Renaissance Villa des Flots, the Persian House, and the Hôtel des Roches Noires are relics of Trouville's golden age. Many of these villas were temporary homes to such artists as Charles Mozin, Paul Huet, Eugène Isabey, Gérard Boudin, and Edouard Manet. More recently, the novelist Marguerite Duras and the poster artist Raymond Savignac lived here. The great landscape artist Camille Corot produced many studies of the region, while Flaubert was inspired by the wife of the owner of the Hôtel Bellevue to create the heroine of his great novel *Sentimental Education*. But it was Marcel Proust who most perfectly captured the ambience of Trouville, writing while still a young man about the Norman houses "where the abundance of finials increases the viewpoints and complicates the silhouette, where the broad windows are blessed with such softness and intimacy, where flowers cascade endlessly from window boxes set into the wall beneath each window over the outside stairs and the glass-sided halls."

Honfleur is something else altogether, although the town still considers itself among the select. Nowadays most of the boats moored here are yachts rather than fishing smacks, but Honfleur is proud of its seagoing heritage. The town dates back to the eleventh century, and its heyday came in the seventeenth century, when Samuel de Champlain, a shipowner from Dieppe, sailed from Honfleur for the New World. De Champlain is considered the discoverer of Canada and the father of Quebec.

Honfleur is a town of great charm. Strolling round the old seventeenth-century port, designed in the neoclassical style by Duquesne, it is easy to imagine the excitement of setting

sail for unknown adventures half a world away. It is delightful to stop in at one of the many cafés for a taste of the local fare: sparkling, cool cider in an earthenware bowl, along with a delicious crêpe. As you explore the old town, visit Erik Satie's home, the tower of Saint Catherine's, and the old, oak-framed, stone salt warehouses on place Arthur-Boudin. Every Saturday morning, place Sainte-Catherine hosts a bustling street market where local farmers come to sell their produce—fresh fruit and vegetables, honey, cheeses, and cider.

In the town center, many of the old half-timbered buildings now house art galleries. Around the old port, between Quai Saint-Etienne and Quai Sainte-Catherine, the style of architecture changes. The homes on Quai Saint-Etienne are in stone and have two floors and an attic. Those on Quai Sainte-Catherine are built of poorer material, and can have as many as seven floors. Their façades are fortified with planks of wood with slates to protect against the elements. This jumble of building materials produces an overall sense of liveliness that is strangely harmonious in tone. The slate gives the town much of its character, as it changes color in accordance with the weather—from a dull steely gray, when storm clouds blow in off the sea, to slick, pearly gray, when the rain has passed and the sun shines once more. Honfleur, lying on the cusp between pays d'Auge and the Côte de Grâce, is an amateur artist's dream.

Houlgate is less well known, but perhaps all the more charming for that very reason. Its golden age was the late nineteenth century, when the great and the good built their weekend villas there. Many of these villas are so well known locally that they don't need addresses, including Les Courlis, Les Sirènes, Le Clos Fleuri, and a clutch of American-inspired villas—Tacoma, Minnehaha, and Columbia. The Villa Jeanne d'Arc has a statue of the maiden saint in a niche on the front façade. Le Carillon is a heady mix of Renaissance, Gothic, and Romanesque architecture, while Beuzeval Manor draws on medieval motifs. Here, the rows of parasols on the beach call to mind the atmosphere of the novels of Thomas Mann. Protected from the sun and the sea breezes, you can pass the hours watching families playing on the beach as you brace yourself for a dip in the chilly waters. Consider an excursion to nearby Villers-sur-Mer, or set out on an expedition to pick the cockles exposed on the rocks at low tide or to search for fossils, plentiful along the Vaches Noires cliffs.

Mention Cabourg, and the name Marcel Proust immediately comes to mind. The great novelist came to this elegant seaside resort to breathe the fresh sea air as a cure for

Above: Port Racine, the smallest port in France, with its stone quays and its boats carefully tied up, as they must be on days when the tide will be at its highest.
Left: The coastal road leading to Port Racine. The cattle browse in pastures that lead right down to the shore.

Above: The Hotel Neptune in Agon-Coutainville, with its balconies looking out over the sea. Normandy's seaside resorts offer a number of hotels with discreet, old-world charm.

Facing page: The Bay of Mont-Saint-Michel. The bay and the mount fully deserve their place on UNESCO's list of World Heritage sites. The church, 262 feet (eighty meters) in length, stands on a rock barely sixty feet (twenty meters) long, resting on four crypts that surround the pinnacle. On the northern side of the monastery, the chancel, refectory, and dormitory are fine examples of Romanesque architecture, while the cloister is a marvel of the Gothic style.

his asthma. His long walks along the beach proved a rich source of information. You can still visit the room he is said to have stayed in beginning in 1881 in the Grand Hôtel. Cabourg is well known today for its Romantic Film Festival—a choice of theme likely inspired by the windy hills above the town that could be straight out of a novel by Emily Brontë. Along the seafront, down from the casino and Grand Hotel, are Cabourg's magnificent villas, many with especially fine gardens full of scented blossoms. Their large bay windows—a feature of many of the villas—reflect the scudding clouds like a Corot landscape.

Nearby Dieppe is more modern in feel than the genteel resorts that reached their peak of fashion in the late nineteenth century. Dieppe is the closest in proximity to Paris of all the Norman seaside resorts and is also the oldest resort in all of France. It is said that Henri III came here in the sixteenth century to treat a painful skin disease. In 1813, before Dieppe became fashionable, Napoleon's sister-in-law, Queen Hortense of Holland, came here to rest and recuperate. The fashion for sea bathing was launched here in 1820 when the Duchess of Berry braved the steeply plunging cliffs and sharp pebbles on the beach to take a dip. The resort, with its casino and racecourse, became a favorite place for a weekend break from the capital. Musicians rubbed shoulders with artists and politicians—among them Camille Saint-Saëns, Alexandre Dumas, Oscar Wilde, Napoleon III, King Louis-Philippe, and Eugène Delacroix. With the opening of train connections in 1843 and the introduction of paid vacations nearly a century later, the coastal resorts became much more accessible to the Parisians in general. In the early days, the train journey took seven hours. The great novelist Emile Zola put this time to good use to imagine the plot of his novel *La Bete Humaine* on one such journey.

Many visitors still come to the Normandy coastal resorts in search of health and relaxation and to enjoy the seawater treatments offered at many spas in the region. The mild climate, the sea air rich in iodine, the relative closeness to Paris, and the wide range of activities make the Normandy coast one of the most popular tourist destinations in all of France. The health benefits of the coast were first recognized in the eighteenth century, when the sea air was even reputed to be a cure for rabies. The nineteenth century saw the flowering of seaside resorts all along the Normandy coast—Carteret, Courseulles-sur-Mer, Hermanville, and Granville, known locally as the Monaco of the North and famous for its sea mud and seaweed treatments rich in trace elements. Luc-sur-Mer is recommended for those suffering from arthritis and general fatigue. Ouistreham is another popular thermal spa.

We end our visit to the Normandy coast in Pont-Audemer, Normandy's answer to Venice. Here lies the soul of Normandy, where a maze of lakes and canals reflect the ever-changing moods of the sky. The charms of the Normandy coast are quiet and refined rather than flashy, but to those who know how to appreciate them, they are all the more enchanting for being so discreet.

The green fields of Normandy

Normandy is known as the garden of France. The limestone, schist, clay, and granite soils, generously watered by abundant showers, give the land a lush cloak of green. Here, a landscape painter needs only three colors—blue, white, and green. Blue for the fields of flax in the pays de Caux, where the plant has grown since the Paleolithic era. Blue for the endless expanse of the sky. White for the apple blossoms that blush a delicate shade of pink in April and May, and for the sea foam riding on the crest of the waves. Green for the fields, forests, and copses complete the enchantment of this distinctive landscape.

There is no escaping the fact that it rains in Normandy, sometimes a lot. The best way to regard the sudden showers is to accept them as heaven's promise that this year's harvest will be bountiful. For without its verdant pastures and fruit-laden orchards, Normandy would lose its essence. The rain offers a chance to explore the countryside undisturbed, to enjoy romantic walks in the forest before returning home to dry out in front of a welcoming fire. If you brave the early morning mists that are a regular feature of the weather, you will discover a mysterious world where the soil seems to exhale delicate veils of dew. When storms threaten, the land takes on a melancholy aspect as the sky casts gray light, from pearl to steel, over the countryside. Georges Seurat captured these landscapes in a minor key in his superb paintings, using a palette of delicate gray hues.

The pays de Bray is an oasis of greenery perched high on the Caux plateau, where the land shrugs off its gentle character in exchange for dramatic hills and plunging valleys. Perhaps the herds of cattle browsing placidly in the fields don't know it, but they feed on some of the finest pastureland in the world. The geological history of the region in the Tertiary period goes some way toward explaining this. On the eastern border of France, the genesis of the Alps set up a geological shock wave that rent the country from east to west as far as Normandy, pushing parts of what is now the Seine-Maritime *département* up to altitudes of some three thousand feet (one thousand meters). But over time, erosion gradually did its work, gnawing away at the land until the dramatic landscapes of prehistory were worn down to the

Left: The mysterious forest of Offranville. Not far away are the splendid gardens of William-Farcy and the kitchen gardens of the château de Miromesnil.
Facing page: Courboyer Manor is a medieval stone fortress complete with tower and bartizans. Dating from the fifteenth century, it is one of the finest examples of a feudal castle to survive in the region.

Right: The village of Veules-les-Roses, on the banks of the Veules, one of France's shortest rivers, just 4,000 feet (1,194 meters) in length. The half-timbered houses and thatched roofs have made this little fishing village a popular destination. Left: The Varenne is just one of the many rivers in this region. The Varenne valley is lined with fields of placidly grazing cows—a typically Norman scene.

Above: Near Lisieux, the château of Saint-Germain-de-Livet, with its checkerboard façade of white stone and green and ocher brick. There is something of the Italian Renaissance about this fifteenth-century château, which stands on the banks of a small stream. Jean de la Varende called it "an ivory château studded with emeralds." Facing page: Dovecotes are found all over Normandy. Top, left: The dovecote at Jehan Ango's manor in Varengeville. Center and right: A dovecote bearing the Offranville coat of arms. Bottom, left to right: a dovecote near Vauville at the furthest tip of the Cotentin; in Auberville-la-Manuel in the pays de Caux; in Bonneville in the pays d'Ouche.

gentle valleys that we associate with the region today. The only reminder of this tormented geological past is the village of Ferté-Saint-Samson, perched on an outcrop at an altitude of six hundred feet (190 meters).

In the pays de Bray, nature reigns supreme. Life passes quietly in these beautiful, gentle valleys where the landscape is dotted with copses and tranquil streams. This is where Delphine Couturier spent her days until she decided to seek excitement in the big city. Her tragic story inspired Flaubert to write what many consider the greatest French novel of the nineteenth century, *Madame Bovary*. His contemporary, Jean Barbey d'Aurevilly, also a Norman by birth, described this land in loving detail: "The heaths suddenly interrupt these fresh, laughing, fertile landscapes with melancholy, an atmosphere of anxiety, a severe look. They cast a blacker shadow over them...."

In Normandy, there has always been a friendly rivalry between the north and the south—although the difference is rather an imagined one, as the landscape barely changes from one end to the other. All of Normandy, however, is blessed with a talent for peace and calm. The "north" is considered to include the western reaches of the Paris basin, where the Seine river flows through deep valleys; while the "south" extends as far east as Brittany. Although the administration prefers the terms Upper and Lower Normandy—without implying a question of superiority or even a difference in altitude—the terms are used purely to describe their geographical location in relation to Paris. Normandy's close proximity to Paris has played a key role in determining its character over the centuries, and the Seine has left its mark on Normandy's landscape and history alike. The river takes its name from either the Latin *sequana* or the Celtic *squan*, terms that mean "winding" or "sinuous." The river may meander through gently sloping valleys, but do not let its quiet demeanor fool you: its current is extremely powerful as it winds its way across the land to the sea. For centuries, the Seine has provided an important trading route for merchants bringing their wares to Paris, enabling fishermen to supply the capital with fresh-caught fish and oysters in the nineteenth century. One of the prettiest sites along the river is the village of Les Andelys, with the ruins of Château Gaillard.

Beyond the Seine valley, the country takes on the familiar aspect every Frenchman associates with picture-postcard Normandy: rich pastures, sleepy manor houses, long, low farmhouses lying on the edge of a copse, and beech forests like the one at Cerisy, where deer and wild boar roam free, their peace disturbed only during the hunting season.

Most of the fertile Normandy farmland is on limestone soil. The land here typically offers fields of waving corn and sweeping views to the horizon with no trees to interrupt the view, particularly around Neubourg and Evreux-Saint-André. Driving past these fields at twilight, one feels as though the world were perfectly flat and featureless until reaching a tiny village of stone houses. In the not too far distant pays de Caux, the landscape changes. Here, the rich soil is composed of clay and flint, which provide plenty of nourishment for the trees crowded on the hillsides and around isolated houses. The land here and as far as the Vexin natural park to the east is used for growing wheat, rape-seed, flax, and sugar beet.

In 1991, the Cotentin and Bessin marshlands were declared a natural park. It is a magical place of utter tranquility, with lakes and meadows, canals where narrow boats glide on smooth waters, isolated copses, and marshes that in winter are flooded into one vast lake. The park is perfect for long winter walks or for cycling tours, boat trips, or even caravan vacations. It is a bewitching landscape, where little wooden boats slip silently through the haze rising off the lakes, and where the stone houses that dot the countryside seem almost abandoned, so quiet is the atmosphere. Here, time seems to stand still; the silence is interrupted only by the occasional cry of the storks, ducks, Montagu's harriers, snipe, egrets, ospreys, and woodcocks that flock to the nature reserve.

One of the most characteristic features of the Normandy countryside is the type of landscape known in French as *bocage*—gently rolling farmland crisscrossed with hedges and copses of broadleaf trees, where apple orchards and ancient hedgerows lie alongside forests where the boar and deer roam free. The *bocage* has been a feature of the land here for centuries, and plays an important role in ensuring the stability of the ecosystem. The farmers here work with an acidic soil that stretches far to the east, as far as the Paris basin. The same type of soil is found further south in the Maine and in Le Perche, and to the west in the Armorican massif in Brittany, as well as in the pays d'Ouche and the pays d'Auge. The pays d'Auge is the sort of countryside that French people are talking about when say they're going for a weekend in Normandy—a rich land of lush, grassy meadows, picturesque half-timbered houses, and majestic old manor homes where life seems to have stood still for centuries. Seen from the air, the countryside around the village of Domfront looks like a giant patchwork of fields patterned by the fruit orchards and hemmed by the darker green of hedges. Domfront itself is famous both for its relatively high altitude—some 650 feet (215 meters) above sea level—and its superb medieval buildings. But its greatest claim to fame is—according to Chrétien de Troyes, who recorded many of the Arthurian legends in poetry in the twelfth century—that it is the birthplace of Sir Lancelot.

Despite its rather fragmented appearance, the *bocage* regions have always been characterized by their powerful sense of place. If the region's farmers did not strongly defend the unique local identity, the patchwork of fields, hedgerows, and copses would have long since been swallowed up into vast, featureless plains, as has happened to many other regions of France. Norman farmers love their land, and are ready to fight to maintain their ancient traditions, from the pays de Bray to the north, with its clay soil and chalk slopes in the Roumois; to the Lieuvin regions, divided by the Risle valley. The river Risle is joined at Serquigny by the Charentonne, a fast-flowing river well stocked with fish. In ancient times, its banks were dotted with waterwheels that powered the local flour mills, forges, and looms; although the passage of time has not always been kind to these charming stone buildings. The Orne

Above: A panoramic view of La Bouille. Most of the houses have terraces looking out over the river or are on the cliff top, offering splendid views over the Seine valley. The town hosts a regatta every summer. In bygone days, there was a regular steamboat service to Rouen, the regional capital.
Left: The château of Carny-Barville in the pays de Caux dates from the sixteenth century and is now protected under heritage laws. The river Durdent flows along one side of the grounds, creating an atmosphere of great serenity.

Above: A wintry sky over the frosty banks of the Risle, near Bec-Hellouin.
Right: The façade of a half-timbered house in Bec-Hellouin. This typically Norman technique was lost during the Renaissance, but was rediscovered in the late nineteenth century. The frame of vertical timbers is filled with a plaster mix consisting of straw and clay.

valley, between Thury-Harcourt and Alençon, is known as Normandy's answer to Switzerland. This thickly wooded region is best visited, as in the olden days, in a horse-drawn coach or brightly painted gypsy caravan. The manors and abbeys boast of the region's proud heritage. The Orne, on the other hand, is a tranquil river, flowing placidly past the old water mills and willows that line its banks. In spring, cherry trees and broom burst into blossom. Canoeists can explore the reaches of the river in summer and winter alike. But the most impressive natural feature without a doubt is Oëtre Rock, standing some 360 feet (118 meters) over the river Rouvre. At the foot of the cliff, a narrow cave—the Fairy Chamber—has a long association with witchcraft. The village of Saint-Céneri-en-Gérei, near Alençon, is another majestic site. In the seventh century, the Italian hermit Cerenicus decided to make his home here amid the eroded rocks. In the nineteenth century, painters such as Corot, Courbet, and Boudin followed suit, drawn by the serenity of the landscape, the picturesque stone houses, the delightful bridges shaded by willows, the ruined château, and the Romanesque church dating from the twelfth century.

The Risle eventually joins the Seine estuary. While visiting, one should see the Vernier marshes, the Brotonne forest, the streams, meadows, copses, and fields full of cows calmly grazing. Normandy's religious heritage is commemorated in the ancient abbeys of Saint-Martin-de-Boscherville, Jumièges, and Bec-Hellouin. At Bec-Hellouin, founded in the eleventh century by an artistocrat, the monks still take a vow of silence, inspired by the example of Saint Francis of Assisi to cast off their earthly possessions and live henceforth in poverty. Even the swans gliding on the river seem to respect the atmosphere of quiet contemplation. The only interruption of this serene ambience is the nearby river Vire, with its impetuously bubbling waters that dance through emerald-green valleys.

The tiny river Oison—just ten miles (seventeen kilometers) long—is one of the shortest rivers in Normandy. It flows from Saint-Amand-des-Hautes-Terres a short distance down to the Seine. In antiquity, seventeen water-mills stood on its banks. Another notable local feature is France's smallest town hall, in a former chapel measuring just 65 square feet (six square meters), in the village of Saint-Germain-de-Pasquier. Not far off is the Sainte-Clothilde spring, rumored to have curative, even miraculous, properties. The river Durdent is particularly well-stocked with trout. It begins its journey in Héricourt-en-Caux and empties into the Atlantic at Veulettes-sur-Mer, having flowed through an enchanting landscape dotted with manors, churches, and dovecotes. The Valmont and Gonzeville valleys also have their fair share of pretty farms and dovecotes, and in Veulettes-sur-Mer the fortifications of the medieval village, long since destroyed by the encroaching waves, can be seen pushing through the seabed when the tide is at its very lowest. Despite their similar names, Veulettes has little in common with the seaside resort of Veules-les-Roses, where, perched between two cliffs, stand charming villas built early in the twentieth century by wealthy Parisians in search of fresh sea air. The region is

Above: A field in Colonard-Corubert in the Le Perche region, where the land is crisscrossed with a patchwork of pastures and hedges. Le Perche, extending over four départements, is rich in rivers and streams, pastureland, ponds, shallow valleys, and forests.
Right: A rich palette of fall colors for this forest in Le Perche.

known for its watercress harvest, abundantly watered by the shortest river in France, which measures only 4,000 feet (1,194 meters) in length.

In recent years, the Le Perche region has come into fashion and is now one of the most desirable areas of France. Lying between the Paris basin and the Armorican massif in Brittany, it is blessed with abundant rains and a rich soil over schist, sandstone, and granite bedrock. The sloping hills are still thickly covered with oak and beech forests and fertile fields draw nourishment from a bed of marl and clay. Much of Le Perche's charm comes from the hills and valleys, which provide a welcome contrast to the endless flat plains of the Beauce to the south. Le Perche has its own natural park, founded in 1998 and comprising half a million acres (182,000 hectares), ideal for walking or horse-riding holidays. September is the mushroom season in the

Le Perche has a long tradition of horse breeding. The Le Pin stud farm in Exmes is famous for its horse trials. The local Percheron horses are much admired. Facing page: The stables at Le Pin stud farm. Above: Top, left to right: The gates to the stud farm; horses on show in the central courtyard; the stud farm's façade of hewn stone. Bottom, left to right: A display of Percheron horses; a horse's tail plaited for a show; the September horse trials.

forests of La Trappe, Réno-Valdieu, and Bellême. In the Avre valley, the lakes and the Château d'Avre invite a moment of quiet contemplation. The serenity of the atmosphere inspired the monks living in the abbey of La Trappe in the seventeenth century to take a vow of silence; to this day, the Trappists are known for their silent worship. There is something truly unspoiled and authentic about this region, its forests, hills, and rivers, and its ancient tradition of sun-dials, many recently restored, such as the ones in Bellême and Longny-au-Perche.

The small town of Mortagne is typical of the region, with its narrow medieval lanes and humble homes huddled together as if for protection. The orange tones of the bricks and roof tiles, very different from the muted browns of the cob and wood houses in the pays d'Auge, stand out brightly against the green surroundings. One of the prettiest villages hereabout is Monceaux on the banks of the Jambée. The exquisite Pontgirard Manor, dating back to the sixteenth century, is set among magnificent gardens that slope down to the river.

Le Perche has long been associated with horses and even has its own breed, the Percheron, a cross between a cob and an Arab thoroughbred. Percherons were first bred during the Crusades, although it was not until 1823 that the first one was born in Normandy itself, in the Orne *département*. This first Norman-born Percheron was christened Jean Le Blanc. Percherons quickly came to win every prize possible for the elegance of their flared nostrils, majestic arching neck, powerful hindquarters, and splendid gray or black color. They were used as draught horses, pulling carts, military vehicles, and even buses in the early twentieth century. Percherons are the undisputed stars of the horse trials held every September at the Le Pin stud farm. Normandy is proud of its stud farms, which bring thousands of tourists to the region every year. Calvados has no fewer than 1,400 stud farms. The Le Pin is in Exmes, to the east of Argentan. Known as the Versailles of the horse-breeding world, it covers nearly 3,000 acres (1,100 hectares), while the trials are held over a total of 27,000 acres (11,000 hectares) of forests, fields, and pathways. Le Pin was founded in 1715 by Jules Hardouin-Mansart, who designed its buildings in the purest traditions of the enlightenment: a façade of white stone and pastel brick with a roof of gray slate. The central courtyard is shaped like a horseshoe; its stables are in pink brick and limestone, with vaulted doors and mullioned win-dows. The gardens were laid out by the most talented landscape gardener of his day, André Le Nôtre. Today, the Le Pin stud farm is classed as France's finest. It breeds both thoroughbreds and white Percherons. Le Pin is also home to an Institute for Equine Studies, a training school, and a racetrack called La Bergerie.

Above, left: The upper floors of the oldest houses jut out over the narrow streets in the medieval heart of Louviers.
Right: A close-up view of a half-timbered façade in Beaumont-en-Auge. The irregular cut of the wood makes the style all the more charming.

Facing page: A street in Rouen with the Cathedral of Notre-Dame in the background. The cathedral's spire is the tallest in France.
Top right: The clock in the ancient heart of Rouen, where the streets are lined with quaint old half-timbered houses. Until 1520, the houses were built with the upper floors leaning out over the street as a way of providing a little extra space. This was particularly valuable in towns like Rouen, where the streets were very narrow.
Bottom right: A façade with ancient paned windows.

Normandy, the garden of France

The gardens of Normandy

*Preceding spread: The Beaumesnil château in
the pays d'Ouche, between Lisieux and Évreux,
is a majestic building dating from the reign of
Louis XIII, complete with a moat, fountains,
and a maze of yew and boxwood hedges.
Above and facing page: The Château of Bonneville,
also in the pays d'Ouche, is renowned for its topiary
chess pieces. The garden, shaded by magnificent
Scots pines, was the creation of the writer Jean
de La Varende.
Following pages: The German journalist
Paula Almquist designed this lovely garden
of grasses, rare flowers, and fruit trees
in Regnéville-sur-Mer, in the Cotentin.*

Normandy is a garden lover's dream come true. It offers
every style of garden one can imagine: French style, English
style, grand parks and humble kitchen gardens, water gardens, and gardens devoted to rare plants. Each garden is
unique, reflecting the character of its creator. Many of the finest gardens
in Normandy are the work of British men and women who fell in love with
this green land and brought their own brand of floral poetry with them.
Normandy's gardens are sometimes harmonious and poetic, sometimes
an exotic symphony of seductive colors and heady perfumes. Their owners generally prefer them not to look too groomed, working in harmony
with nature rather than trying to dominate it. Yet this apparent neglect is
more often than not the result of many hours of hard work and careful planning. The seemingly haphazard beds throw up unexpectedly beautiful
combinations of colors, shapes, and scents.

In Normandy, gardening has been considered an art form for centuries and is truly part of the region's history and character. The oldest
gardens in Normandy were founded in Gaillon by the archbishop of
Rouen in 1502. A number of famous artists and writers chose Normandy as their home, devoting almost as much time and attention to their gardens as they did to their artwork. Claude
Monet, James McNeill Whistler, and Guy de Maupassant are just three of the best known.
They poured their energies into the banks of rhododendrons, magnolias, hydrangeas, rose gardens, elegant smooth lawns and perfectly trimmed hedges, and mirrored, unruffled ponds. They
painted and wrote about the lustrous dawn and the amethyst hues of twilight. Their gardens
tell us a great deal about the kind of men they were.

At Bonneville, his estate near Le Chamblac, just outside Bernay, the writer and gardener
Jean de La Varende (1887–1959) created a fabulous park of topiary pines and yews punctuated with classical statuary, in homage to the theatricality of Italian Renaissance gardens. De La
Varende fell under the spell of the pays d'Ouche, naming one of his novels after the region. His
Louis XIII château is set in an English-style park, which he planted with a topiary yew garden pruned
in the shape of chess pieces ready for a game. The kings, queens, bishops, and rooks are
trimmed every year. Beyond the strict rows of these plant sculptures is a verdant backdrop of Scots
pines whose luxuriant foliage contrasts strikingly with the clean lines of yews.

The Normandy climate allows all kinds of plants to flourish here, and gardeners have succeeded in transplanting the most unlikely plants from far-flung corners of the globe in this rich earth—plants that hungrily push their roots down into the nutritious loam. Blue poppies from the Himalayas, white birches from China, hellebores from Turkey and the Caucasus, and, above all, rhododendrons, originally from India. But however different the style of plants, one thing unites all of the gardens of Normandy—a deep-seated respect for nature in all her splendor. Sometimes, a garden will take its basic theme from one particular plant, a tree or a rare flower. William Farcy's quiet, introspective garden in Offranville is a fine example. As the Duke of Harcourt once wrote, "A garden that does not inspire one with a sense of serenity loses its *raison d'être*."

The finest gardens in Normandy are not always in private hands. Some of the bigger towns have their own splendid parks, providing a tranquil haven of greenery for the urban population. The gardens of Rouen were created in 1691 by Louis de Carel. First known as the Trianon Park, their name was later changed to the Planterose Gardens. The beds are planted with three thousand species of trees and flowers, with another five thousand more delicate species in the greenhouses. One of the most spectacular is the Amazonian water lily known as Victoria Regia, whose leaves can measure up to three feet (one meter) across in the summer months. Like the glowworms that light up the gloaming, the flowers of this giant lily last only one day. It unfurls its immaculate petals as the sun rises, takes on a soft pink flush at midday, and withers as dusk falls, its petals by then a striking shade of carmine.

Cherbourg is known for its palm trees, but also boasts a fine display of pines and gunnera, or giant rhubarb, on the grounds of the hospital. The Emmanuel-Liais Park, in the Bucaille district of Cherbourg, is named after an adventurer who explored Brazil in the nineteenth century, bringing back plants that still proliferate in the garden that bears his name. This remarkable collection of exotic plants is rivaled by another garden nearby, La Roche-Fauconnière, which boasts no fewer than four thousand rare species. In Caen, the park on the Colline aux Oiseaux, the birds' hill, where seagulls nest, has matured into an elegant rose garden with the finest roses of yesteryear alongside more modern varieties. The fifty acres (twenty hectares) of the park include a number of exotic gardens, a picturesque wisteria walk, and a boxwood maze.

Whether in town centers or in the heart of the country; on the coast or on the edge of a forest, the gardens of Normandy share one common feature—they reflect the loving care lavished upon them by gardeners who have sought to enhance a corner of nature. Many times I have found myself standing transfixed with wonder in such a garden, knowing that the waves of the Atlantic were breaking on the shore just a hundred feet away but imagining myself in the garden of Eden.

English inspiration

A floral symphony on the grounds of the Bois des Moutiers, and the Shamrock garden in Varengeville. The Bois des Moutiers is known for its spectacular display of rhododendrons, which flower for just a few weeks from mid-May to early June—but the sight is worth the wait.

The British have always had something of a soft spot for Normandy, probably because so many aspects of life here remind them of their homeland: the gentle landscape, the frequent rain showers, the clouds scudding across the sky, and the opportunity for long walks across the fields or along the beach, followed by a warming drink by the fire. They feel quite at home here. In recent years, many English families have moved across the Channel, enticed by a better quality of life, to make Normandy their new home. They have brought with them the untamed poetry of their gardens, often said to be the loveliest in the world, precisely because they leave part of the work in the capable hands of nature. It comes as something as a surprise to realize that the phenomenon of the British influence on the landscape is not a new one. Guy de Maupassant, writing in the nineteenth century, noted: "The open countryside in Normandy, rolling and melancholy, resembles an immense English park." Norman gardeners have always sought inspiration across the Channel and even made trips to bring back particular plant specimens. The Countess de Vogüé, for example, who created the delightful kitchen garden at the Château de Miromesnil, never missed the Chelsea Flower Show. Martine Lemonnier often visited the Botanical Gardens in Edinburgh to bring back ideas—and seedlings—for her nursery, while Princess Sturdza loved Knightshayes Park in Devon.

English-style gardens may be characterized by their look of studied neglect, but the effect is in fact carefully planned. Each shrub, tree, flower, and leaf is chosen to look its best in all seasons, settings, and from all vantages. A touch of irregularity prevents the overall effect from becoming too perfect and characterless. The English like their gardens to have a sense of architectural structure—a towering cypress to break up the straight line of the horizon, stepped terraces, curving branches matching the fluid lines of the flowerbeds and providing a sense of continuity from one part of the garden to another. The climbing plants, hardy perennials, and shrubs are fed on a mixture of soil, peat, and manure. Some plants are selected for their neutral colors, providing a subtle backdrop to the brilliant flamboyance of a carefully chosen blossom. Water, terraces, hedges, and slopes are all key ingredients in an English-style garden. The overall effect is one of a series of enclosed, independent spaces linked by an overarching sense of harmony, light, and balance. At their best, such gardens put on an equally magnificent display whatever the season.

One particularly fine example of the influence of the English style of gardening is the Bois des Moutiers garden in Varengeville-sur-Mer. Nothing in this splendid garden was left

to chance, and the result is truly sublime. One can almost believe that the garden had been touched by the hand of God, like Adam on the ceiling of the Sistine chapel. Not a hint of the strenuous effort it takes to tend such a garden—or of the havoc occasionally wrought by storms—is evident. This garden was nothing but open fields until Guillaume Mallet, enchanted by its beauty and with an eye to its artistic potential, purchased the estate at the end of the nineteenth century. Inspired by his numerous visits to English gardens—on the Isle of Wight in particular—he set about re-creating their bucolic atmosphere in this corner of Normandy. The acid soils were ideal for all kinds of plants. He planted camellias, azaleas from China, Japanese maples, eucryphias from Chile, and hydrangeas. Most spectacular of all are the banks of Himalayan rhododendrons that stand over twenty-five feet (eight meters) tall and are at their most vibrant in May and June. The thirty acres (twelve hectares) of the estate slope gently down toward the waters of the Atlantic, with the sea wind often sweeping in over the grounds, bringing a fine mist of salt spray.

The garden is constructed on a thematic scheme. The first is a garden of pure white flowers, ringed by a protective yew hedge. Followed by beds of low box hedges scattered with tulips, lilies, roses, and hellebores. A little further on stands a pergola overgrown with jasmine and wisteria vines and a sundial framed with Ballerina roses. Beyond the sundial are a cluster of magnolias and a rose garden in what was once the kitchen garden. The house and grounds were designed in 1898 by the great architect Edwin Lutyens in collaboration with the renowned gardener Gertrude Jekyll, and represent the earliest experiment in France of the Arts and Crafts movement, then in its infancy. The work was complicated, however, by the fact that Lutyens and Jekyll had very different views on how the garden should look: Edwin wanted a wide-open space in harmony with the architecture of the house; Gertrude preferred a garden divided into a number of quadrants, each coming into its own as the seasons changed. She planned gardens of bulbs for spring, roses for summer, and asters for fall.

Guillaume Mallet followed Jekyll's advice in designing his "wild garden," where roses, lilies-of-the-valley, shrubs, strawberry trees, holm oaks, maples, and beech trees were allowed to grow unchecked to form a dramatic backdrop to the banks of Halopeanum rhododendrons, said to be the tallest and most spectacular in the region.

Above: At the Bois des Moutiers, an avenue of azaleas set against a dramatic, dark background of Atlas cedars. Facing page: A succession of walled gardens ending in a pergola designed by Gertrude Jekyll— a haven for the Lykkefund, Rosa Willmottiae, and Francis E. Lester roses that grow in profusion at the far end of the garden.

60

Left: The grounds of Pontrancart Château in Seine-Maritime, where the flowers bloom between mid-August and mid-September. The beds are planted with annuals, bulbs, and hardy perennials. The garden was laid out by the landscape architect Lloyd Jones early in the twentieth century.
Right: The maze by the château. Yew hedges enclose a series of small gardens, each planted with flowers of a different color.

So the park changes from season to season, but remains dazzlingly beautiful, even in the dead of winter when, on frosty days, and when the winter sun shines bright, the needles of the blue cedars nearly match the peerless blue of the sky.

The well-known English gardener Russell Page also left his mark on a number of gardens throughout Normandy, including Pontrancart, in the pays de Caux, and the Varaville stud farm near Cabourg, which he designed in 1966. At Pontrancart, the shrubs and plants all burst into flower in a spectacular display that lasts just one short month—from mid-August to mid-September. The grounds are laid out like a maze, with splashes of red, yellow, and blue linked by banks of white Iceberg roses to harmonize the effect. The avenues lined with linden trees offer refreshing shade to the fruit trees growing between them, while shrubs of spring flowers enliven the lawns. Beds of white and pink flowers, lavender, silver-leafed shrubs, banks of acanthus, hawthorn bushes, and wild apple trees dot the garden. All in all, the garden is a vibrant homage to the generosity of nature.

The spirit of the Enlightenment

Above: The grounds of the Château de Canon, near Caen. The avenues of statues inspired by Greek and Roman mythology give the gardens a dream-like atmosphere.
Facing page: The façade has a superb gallery of Italianate balusters reflected in the lake. The grounds are a blend of French and English influences. The owner, Elie de Beaumont, a friend of Voltaire, created this garden shortly after the French Revolution. He was inspired by contemporary English theories on landscaping.

The Normandy countryside is scattered with sleepy old mansion houses, their façades weathered by time and often demurely hidden behind a veil of ivy. Their gardens are havens of peace and tranquility that invite the visitor to pause and contemplate her surroundings, while delicate perfumes caress her senses. Some owners prefer their gardens untamed; a bohemian blend of azaleas and various blossoms, shrubs, and exotic trees. Others prefer the strict lines of geometrical flower beds in the French style, with avenues of plane trees and lindens laid out straight, as if with a ruler, carefully planned copses and vistas, and trees shaped and trimmed as if with a hairdresser's scissors. However, it is rare to find a garden hereabouts that has not had its strictness softened by a touch of the British influence, with the addition of a pagoda, a temple of Venus, a fake ruin, or another such ivy-draped folly. The parks of Normandy's châteaux are an artful combination of restraint and extravagance, strict classicism and anarchy. The garden designed by Elie de Beaumont in the eighteenth century for his estate at the Château de Canon, near Caen, is a fine example of that principle. De Beaumont, a frequent visitor to England, was particularly impressed by the great gardens of Stowe and Kew, and brought many of the ideas he found there to his estate. The great gates of the Château de Canon open onto a broad avenue of linden trees and horse chestnuts. Originally, the grounds were planted with vines, vegetable patches, and fruit orchards alongside ponds and copses. There was a Chinese pagoda taken from the Château du Tertre in Paris, and a temple built by de Beaumont in memory of his late wife. The apple, peach, pear, almond, and fig orchards have since been replaced by beds of dahlias, pansies, and heleniums.

In the nearby gardens of Thury-Harcourt, the key words are classical rigor. This was the case not only in the layout of the flower beds and lawns, but also in the vision of the man behind the garden, the Duke of Harcourt. He believed in "unity of composition, and a maximum of effects obtained with the least input." At Champ-de-Bataille, the tone is equally classical. The gardens here were designed in accordance with the principles put forth by the great eighteenth-century landscape architect André Le Nôtre. The famous Parisian decorator Jacques Garcia, best known for his re-creation of interiors described in Proust's novels, was inspired by mythology in his designs.

Other châteaux in the region have equally dramatic gardens: Beaumesnil, for example, which lies halfway between Lisieux and Evreux, just a stone's throw from the Risle valley. The château and gardens were long known as the Norman Versailles, although the site is

actually far older, dating back to the Crusades. The main part of the château is in the Louis XIII style. The brick façades, Florentine in style, harmonize perfectly with the splendor of the grounds, which have not changed in the slightest since they were designed in the eighteenth century, including the small lake in front of the château. The gardens were the work of one of Le Nôtre's pupils. They are rich in delightful little spots, such as the island where the old medieval keep has been replaced by a boxwood maze, where visitors can spend a charming hour or two finding their way in and out of the tall hedges. An avenue of linden trees and the Lady's rose garden are equally enchanting.

In the heart of the Bessin region, just a few miles from the coast, lies the Château de Brécy in the village of Saint-Gabriel-Brécy, near Bayeux. These grounds are a superb example of early-Renaissance influence on a late medieval garden. They are believed to have been designed by Jules Hardouin-Mansart, although the archives have yet to provide definite proof. The terraced gardens are tapestries of blossoms, framed by superb baroque enclosures decorated with elegant balusters. The estate is famous for its monumental, seventeenth-century gates at the principal entrance, which, gazing up from the bottom of the steps, looks like the gateway to heaven. Walking through these superb gates, the first thing you see is an old cider press to the right, followed by a small herb garden where the scents of thyme, mint, tarragon, and rosemary mingle in the air. Then there are five Italianate terraces, linked by stone steps, with a pond at each level; topiary boxwood sculptures, based on eighteenth-century drawings by the architect André Mollet; secret gardens; a rose garden; and a delightful kitchen garden. As you leave the gardens behind, you spy an ancient baker's oven to the right. A little further on, a thirteenth-century church is nearly hidden behind a screen of leaves.

The gardens of the Château de Sassy—influenced by the poetry of the Italian Renaissance—are more formal, but no less enchanting. The estate lies on the outskirts of Saint-Christophe-le-Jajolet in the Orne valley, near Argentan. The gardens were planned by the landscape architect Achille Duchêne, who was undoubtedly inspired by Le Nôtre's teachings on perspective. The garden was originally a humble vegetable patch before Duchêne set to work transforming it. Its sumptuous green tapestry of lawns and flower beds is edged by a moat

Above: The ponds, walks, and hedgerows of fruit trees at the Château de Canon make for a serene and romantic setting.
Facing page: The avenue of linden trees and horse chestnuts leading up to the château provides an arching bower of cool greenery.

Left, top: Beaumesnil Château, near Evreux. A flower bed ornamented with a trimmed box hedge beneath a brick arcade.
Left, bottom: The moat at Beaumesnil, reflecting a topiary yew tree.
Right: A detail of the flower beds with the trimmed box hedge—a fine example of eighteenth-century style.

and hedges of yew and linden. The walkways through the gardens are made of crushed brick and pink sand, harmonizing pleasantly with the château's façade (behind which lies the largest private library in France). Beyond the garden proper, the grounds extend for 2,500 acres (a thousand hectares), including wildflower meadows and a forest of blue cedars, pleasantly cool in the summer months when the sun filters through the needles.

The Château de Miromesnil in Offranville, just outside Dieppe, is perhaps better known for the château itself than for its gardens, as the writer Guy de Maupassant is believed to have been born here in 1850. While this has not been established beyond a doubt, it is known that he spent at least part of his childhood here. In his story *Le Horla* he wrote, "I love this land, because this is where I have my roots … the roots that attach a man to the land where his forefathers were born and died, that attach him to what people there think and eat, their customs and their food, the local way of speaking … the scent of the earth, the villages, and of the air itself." Today, the château belongs to Thierry de Vogüé and his wife Simone. The grounds are as magnificent as one would expect, but Simone admits she has a soft spot for the kitchen garden in particular, whose very humbleness makes a change after the splendor of the main gardens. But, more importantly, she planned and planted it herself

to feed her young family during World War II. Sheltered by a wall of dusky rose bricks, square patches are planted with cabbages, mint, sage, chives, and other herbs, with a cluster of fruit trees in one corner. Each season brings forth its yield of fresh produce—lettuce and runner beans in June, turnips and celery in July, potatoes and carrots in August, horseradish and corn in September, Brussels sprouts in November, and chicory in December. Beyond the wall, the impressive main gardens flaunt their displays of clematis, roses, magnolias, peonies, bellflowers, and delphinium, which draw visitors from far and wide. The estate is surrounded by grounds of over 8,500 acres (3,500 hectares). Visitors exploring the park may stumble across the modest little chapel dating from the sixteenth century, whose plain sandstone-and-flint exterior gives no clue to the sumptuously decorated interior. In the heart of the park stands a cedar of Lebanon that has provided shade for weary walkers for over three hundred years.

Above: The majestic entrance to the Château de Brécy, between Bayeux and Caen, in the snow. It is believed that the garden was designed by Mansart in the seventeenth century, based on a marquetry pattern. The symmetry and shapes are the essence of grace, typical of the grand French tradition.

Facing page: The intertwining boxwood hedges, as delicate as embroidery, are based on drawings by the eighteenth-century landscape architect André Mollet, who wrote a book on garden design.

Left: The grounds of the Château de Sassy in the heart of the Argentan plain. Its superb bed, planted with a pattern of low boxwood hedges, faces the château's three terraces, which are linked by stairs.
Right: The grounds were laid out in 1910 as a kind of kitchen garden that consisted of a series of small plots edged with fruit trees. The pond in the center of the kitchen garden still exists; in fact, the whole garden is planned around it, creating a vision of delicate precision.

Above: The grounds and façade of the Château de Miromesnil, near Dieppe. These gardens are best known for their annual display of delphiniums, which grow alongside phlox, hosta, and yarrow. Japanese anemones and dahlias brighten up the flower beds with their sunny colors.
Left: The kitchen garden. The château's former owner, Simone de Vogüé, chose to plant a mix of flowers, vegetables, fruit, and herbs. The garden supplied the kitchens with potatoes, corn, squash, strawberries, red currants, black currants, mint, sage, and chives.

Water gardens

Above: Claude Monet's garden in Giverny, near Vernon. In front of the house, the flower beds are neatly divided by gravel walks.
Right: The water garden is a magical sight.

Normandy is never likely to suffer from drought. There is water everywhere: in the rain clouds that can gather in the blink of an eye, the abundant rivers and ponds, and the sea spray, flung up by breakers crashing over the shore. Many of Normandy's loveliest gardens play with water in the form of ponds, streams, and fountains. Marcel Proust called water gardens "floating flower beds," writing that "water gives blooms a more precious color than the color of the blooms themselves."

The eminent landscape designer Russell Page believed that running water tended to suggest quickness and lightness of movement, while still water created a more thoughtful, contemplative mood. The gardens at Beaurepaire, in Martinvast, near Cherbourg, illustrate both of these possibilities. The marshlands that once surrounded the house have been drained and transformed into a forested water garden complete with ponds and cascades.

Driving west from Paris, practically the first village in Normandy one comes upon is the world-famous Giverny. Claude Monet's garden is actually rather unusual as Normandy gardens go. However, the gardens and his superb paintings still bring hordes of visitors here every year, putting Giverny firmly on the art lover's map.

The house is just as enchanting as the garden, with its pink façade and green shutters, overgrown with geraniums, rose bushes, and ivy. Monet bought the house and garden in 1883, despite the rather chilly welcome he received from the locals reluctant to see their way of life disturbed. The lily pond, fringed with yellow and blue irises, azaleas, mauve honesty, and yellow laburnum, proved inspirational. He wrote, "Suddenly, I had the revelation of the magical atmosphere of the pond. I got out my palette, and since then, I have scarcely called on any other models." He painted the garden in all seasons and at all times of day, capturing its enchanting essence on canvases that are known and loved throughout the world. Strolling through the Japanese-inspired water garden, where white and pink water lilies float lazily, crossing the little arched bridge, and wandering through clumps of bamboo and past the rhododendrons, you feel as if you were walking through one of the paintings themselves. It is easy to forget that the garden is the result of a lot of hard work.

A local stream, the Ru, was diverted to flow beneath the Japanese bridge overhung with wisteria and shaded by a weeping willow. Up by the house, the more traditional flower garden is perhaps less enchanting, but still beautiful. Monet chose to keep the yews that stood in the garden, planting more exotic species alongside them, such as a Japanese flowering cherry and a Japanese apple tree. He also planned the romantic bowers overgrown with climbing roses and clematis. He disliked the idea of strictly regimented flowers in straight rows in their beds, preferring to sow unexpected combinations of flowers and using the greenery of the hedges as a backdrop. He was particularly fond of wildflowers, peonies, and irises. The garden proved to be an extremely time consuming and expensive hobby, but it was a wise investment, allowing him to produce his famous paintings of haystacks, poplar trees, and water lilies.

As time passed, Giverny drew a number of important artists, whose names read like a roll call of the art world in the last years of the nineteenth century—including Berthe Morisot, Gustave Caillebotte, and Camille Pissarro. Among the American artists to visit were Willard Metcalf, John Singer Sargent, and Lilla Cabot Perry. Giverny also became home to writers and actors such as Paul Valéry and Sacha Guitry. The Claude Monet Foundation renovated the house in 1966; now it is a charming little museum, while the garden is exactly the same as when Monet himself tended it.

The Château de Nacqueville, lying on the coast between La Hague and Cherbourg, may be less famous than Giverny, but it is just as romantic. A sixteenth-century manor house with a superb neoclassical façade decorated with turrets, it was once home to Hippolyte de Tocqueville, brother of Alexis, the famous nineteenth-century historian. Visitors enter the manor by means of a drawbridge; a few mighty sequoias still stand in the park, a relic of the manor's former owner who brought them back from America. The garden is an homage to the Romantic age, with cascading rivers, fountains, beech groves, banks of rhododendrons, and a picturesque pond. The river Castellets, which flows through the park, adds to the magic. The ground's eighty-six acres (thirty-five hectares), which slope gently down toward the Atlantic, were designed in 1830 by an English landscape architect. In 1880, the château became the property of a certain Hildevert Hersent, who set about increasing the number of cascades, calming the impetuous waters of the stream to a gently flowing river lined with arum lilies, purple rhododendrons, azaleas, hortensias, and camellias.

Water gardens are always enchanting places to while away a few hours, with the sunlight dappling the surface and the soft music of the ripples. The eighteenth-century artist Louis de Carmontelle wrote, "Water is a moving dream, a pleasing dream, that amuses us

Above: Claude Monet's water garden. Lush vegetation gives the garden something of the appearance of a jungle. The banks are linked with iris, azaleas, rhododendrons, and laburnum.

Facing page: The garden is best known for the water lilies that float on the lake. Monet painted the Japanese bridge on a number of occasions. The metal arch is softened by the overhanging branches of a white-blossomed wisteria that in the summer provide a screen of lacy blooms. The garden creates a mood of contemplation. Monet wrote that in the garden, "The effect varies from one minute to the next…. The heart of the motif is the mirror of water whose aspect changes thanks to the skies reflected in it, spreading life and movement."

with its illusions." Amateur gardeners who settle on a water garden often have rather eclectic tastes in plants, preferring trees and rare species of flowers to ordinary flower beds, and delighting in the poetry of streams and cascades, yew mazes, climbing roses, and fountains in unexpected corners.

The Château de Vendeuvre boasts one such garden, yet it is best known for its superb grotto decorated with two hundred thousand shells.

Then there is the Château de Bizy, a stone's throw from Vernon, where the grounds subtly combine classicism with whimsy. The park was designed in the eighteenth century in the most ostentatious French style, with ornamental flower beds, gravel walkways, and avenues of rigidly symmetrical trees. The Marshal of Belle-Isle and his wife were proud to receive Louis XV and Madame de Pompadour at a superb celebration held in their honor here. A few years later, once royalty had been restored after the revolution, King Louis-Philippe transformed the grounds into an English garden. Today, its key features are an avenue lined with impressive linden trees and the water garden with its fountain statues of horses pawing the air in their center. The designer was the great eighteenth-century master Constant d'Ivry, who came up with a revolutionary new system to feed the fountains by drawing water from local streams. The water trickles from the springs down steps leading into the basin of the fountain, frothing around the horse sculptures before flowing beneath the stables, through the trough where the horses' hooves were washed, and beneath the château itself, finishing its journey in a second fountain, decorated with antique columns, and on to the river a few yards further on. The water thus flowed down from the springs in the village of Bizy above the château, across the park, and into the Seine.

Left: The Château de Nacqueville in the Cotentin. The grounds, laid out in 1830, are planted with rhododendrons, azaleas, and heather. Above: The Castellets river winds its way across a lawn planted with arum lilies.

Flower gardens

Paula Almquist's garden is protected by Regnéville-sur-Mer harbor, the largest of the eight harbors in the Cotentin. This place is born of the meeting of the sea's salt water and the fresh water of the river Sienne.
Above: The house set in its pretty gardens.
Facing page: Paula Almquist has planted grasses, rare flowers, and fruit trees in her garden. The village church can be seen in the background. The Atlantic occasionally sends salt spray and mist rolling in over the garden.

It is often said that gardening is one of the fastest-growing hobbies in the world. Whether you have a couple of acres or a couple of window boxes, there are very few things more satisfying than watching your lovingly tended plants spring into bloom. Some gardening enthusiasts, however, are not content just to enjoy the same ordinary flowers their neighbors have. These are the true collectors, not hesitating to travel the length and breadth of the country—or even to the world—to find a rare specimen. The French National Conservatory of Plant Species keeps records of a number of gardens in Normandy that possess just such gems. The most important is without a doubt Princess Sturdza's collection of rhododendrons in her estate gardens at Vasterival, in Sainte-Marguerite-sur-Mer, near Varengeville. In fact, the princess herself instigated the fashion for such exotic plant collections. In the eighteenth century, a new species of rhododendron from the East Coast of the United States was introduced in Britain and Normandy. The highly decorative shrub proved to be perfectly acclimatized to unpredictable Norman weather, particularly the frequent rains. The Vasterival collection is at its finest between February and May, when the rhododendrons planted alongside hellebores, skimmias, hydrangeas, and magnolias come into bloom. The magnolias are also remarkable, with certain varieties flowering only every sixteen years. The garden is also scattered with charming wildflowers—violets, heather, and ferns. The princess made it a rule to respect the natural look of the garden, refusing to impose any artificial features or superfluous ornamentation. She insisted on leaving nature a free hand with the bulbs, hardy perennials, shrubs, crocuses, and witch hazel that grew haphazardly in the gardens.

Roses are another favorite for collectors. Angélique's Garden at Montmain, near Rouen, was created by Gloria and Yves Le Bellegard, in memory of their much-loved daughter—an enchanting floral homage to a girl who adored old-fashioned roses, apple trees, and bowers of pastel blossoms. The seventeenth-century manor stands at the heart of a superb rose garden with more than two thousand varieties of blooms. The owner of the Château de Bellevue, just outside Tôtes, between Dieppe and Rouen, shares this passion for roses. Martine Lemonnier specializes in hellebores, also known as Christmas roses. Her collection has entered the record books as one of the largest in Europe.

The Normandy climate is particularly kind to geraniums. Colette Sainte-Beuve is a keen collector, with a large area devoted to geraniums in her garden in Plantbessin-Castillon, between Bayeux and Saint-Lô. The garden as a whole is planned around seven themes. The Forrières-du-Bosc estate in Seine-Maritime also has a superb display of geraniums.

Some of Normandy's loveliest gardens do not specialize in one particular species, preferring a range of colors, shapes, and perfumes. The remarkable charm of Paula Almquist's garden on the cliffs above Regnéville-sur-Mer lies in the carefully crafted visual impact of square beds edged with banks of leafy shrubs. She is fortunate in having a stunning setting for her land, looking out over the church tower in the village down below, and, in the near distance, the Atlantic ocean. Almquist is a German journalist who years ago fell under the spell of this corner of Normandy, caressed by the sea breeze. She is a keen collector of exotic grasses, rare flowers, and fruit trees. But her collection has a long way to go to match that of the Château de Vauville in the village of Beaumont-Hague, near the Nez de Jobourg headlands. The gardens of this imposing manor house boast more than seven hundred rare plants, all natives of the southern hemisphere. Fortunately, the strong winds that sweep this stretch of the Cotentin coast do not seem to have an adverse effect on these fragile plants, which are protected by natural windbreaks in the form of hedges and leafy screens. The botanical collection was begun in 1947 by Nicole and Eric Pellerin and is now in the hands of their son Guillaume and his wife Cléophée de Turckheim. The most delicate flowers—arum lilies, agapanthus, artemisia, and camellias—are protected from the wind by natural screens of eucalyptus, escallonias, and cypress. Over the years, Guillaume Pellerin has also put together a remarkable collection of antique gardening tools. The garden is a superb homage to the power of nature to adapt, with fragile, exotic flowers from the other side of the world growing alongside sturdy native plants. The garden was honored in 1992 when it was awarded the legal status of a protected historic monument.

One thing all of these gardens have in common is a respect for nature and a certain humility. This is something that landscape architect Louis Benech feels very strongly about. One of his most ambitious projects was the garden of the Saint-Michel priory near Vimoutiers, in the heart of the pays d'Auge, where he came up with a design in four dominant colors, white, pink, yellow, and red. He claims: "I feel ill at ease with people who make extravagant demands that do not fit the character of their gardens, or who see them as just another status symbol." The garden he produced for the priory was based on the very simple principle of matching the design to the character of the site. The result was a symphony of roses, irises, hardy perennials, and herbs, framed by a discreet walkway lined with magnificent linden trees.

If further proof were needed of the generosity of Normandy's soil and climate, the Coudray estate in Étaimpuis, between Dieppe and Rouen, provides ample confirmation.

Left: Princess Sturdza's Vasterival garden in Sainte-Marguerite-sur-Mer, near Varengeville. The garden follows the contours of the land. The avenue is lined with maples, Japanese flowering cherries, and shadberry trees. The grounds are planted with hellebore, hydrangeas, and magnolias.

Facing page: The Château de Vauville's gardens at the furthest reaches of the Cotentin. The temperate microclimate means that despite strong winds that blow in off the ocean, palm trees, cypresses, eucalyptus, and arum lilies all grow here.

Top, right: The sixteenth-century fortress and the twelfth-century keep.

Bottom, right: The contrast between the medieval walls and the sub-tropical palm trees is striking.

Right, bottom: The priory of Saint-Michel near Vimoutiers, in the pays d'Auge, welcomes visitors. The ivy-clad façade dates from the twelfth century.
Right, top: The pond at the priory of Saint-Michel, with water plants, irises, and grasses growing around it.
Left: The rose garden, designed in 1989 by Louis Benech, is planted with Milrose, Ballerina, and Gallica roses. The beds are grouped according to color and perfume.

Just fifteen or so miles from the coast, the microclimate that arises as the sea breezes blow inland helps the gardens to flourish. Thanks to this exceptional microclimate, the Coudray estate has managed to transplant over six thousand different plant species, from China, the Andes, Australia, and Japan. These exotic foreign species flourish alongside native plants such as holly and other shrubs. The rose garden is exceptional, flowering all year round. The botanist Jean le Bret is especially proud of his collection of primroses and ferns planted on the banks of a stream. To visitors, however, the most remarkable testimony to his patience and skill is that all of the exotic plants he has brought back from his travels throughout the world seem to have settled very happily in this corner of northwestern France.

The English gardener Mark Brown is another foreigner who has happily adapted to Norman soil. Along with being a much-respected gardener and landscape architect, he is also a keen watercolorist. His love of painting shines through in his gardens, each of which is as colorful as his artwork. He draws sustenance from his daily contact with nature, finding inspiration in the design of bark peeling from a tree, the poetry of a fallen leaf, or the delicate tint of a petal. Among his finest creations are the gardens at Ango Manor in Varengeville, which he designed in the late 1980s. The picturesque, half-timbered manor house is set in a meadow beside an orchard of cider apples. The key feature is the walled garden of white flowers; beyond that, Brown decided to leave the wildflowers growing in the meadow, believing nature to be the greatest artist of all. He also planted beds of pink, purple, and blue flowers, sowing the plants in unexpected combinations, so that geraniums and asters grow beneath maples alongside hydrangeas with white lacy petals, dwarf bamboos, and Japanese primroses. On the far side of the manor house, the scenery changes. Here, the dominant colors are pastel grays, blues, apricot, salmon, and bronze—a choice of tones inspired by memories of sunsets in his native town of Newhaven in England. These subtle colors are picked up again in the santolinas, artemisias, chrysanthemums, and meadow saffron that dot the garden. There is also a delightful blue flower called *Ceanothus impressus* that gives off the aroma of fresh gingerbread. In front of the house is the Shakespeare Garden, where Brown has planted all the flowers he associates with the tragic figure Ophelia. Many flowers have a particular meaning in the language of flowers—rosemary

Above, top: Mark Brown's house in Varengeville. The plants are predominantly white and green, including grasses, maples, dwarf bamboos, and Japanese primroses. Above, bottom: The orchard with its skillfully planned beds. Right: The wall of pastel-toned poppies, euphorbia, and irises is typically English in character.

Far left: Christian Dior's garden at the Villa les Rhumbs in Granville. Beneath the wooden veranda lies a patio with climbing roses and a pond lined with papyrus.
Left: The rose garden created by Christian Dior's mother. The bowers are delightfully cool in the heat of summer.
Right: The Villa les Rhumbs was built by the shipbuilder Beust in 1895. The rather unusual name is a naval term that means a constant direction followed on a nautical compass. Maurice and Madeleine Dior, parents of Christian, bought the villa in 1905. In 1997, it became a museum retracing the history of fashion from 1900 to the present.

and pansies for remembrance, daisies and violets for tenderness, Madonna lilies for faith, apothecary roses for melancholy. The flower beds along the walls of the house are a riot of color, from carmine to royal purple, blue, orange, and yellow. These beds are planted with asters, meadow saffron, sage, verbena, euphorbias, and oriental hellebores.

The Plume garden in Auzouville-sur-Ry boasts a fine collection of grasses. The owners Sylvie and Patrick Quibel explain: "We have planted grasses everywhere, in the meadows, the copses, and on the slopes. What we like about grasses is that they give the garden a certain sense of freedom that went out of fashion in the 1970s. We enjoy mixing hardy perennials with grasses people would normally consider weeds, creating the illusion of a beautiful wild garden." All of their plants are for sale—old-fashioned roses, herbs, hardy perennials, water plants, and their collection of clematis.

The garden is based around five themes that follow the seasons. The Plume garden is described as "a series of ripples of light plants waving in the wind, their flowers like sea spray." In this part of the garden, some of the exotic grasses stand more than six feet (two meters) tall. The southern garden is more classical in style, with trimmed box hedges and flowers in shades of scarlet, yellow, orange, and bronze. Here, the Quibels have planted dahlias, heleniums, euphorbia, and poppies. In the fall garden to the west of the house there are asters, chrysanthemums, geraniums, and clematis flower in early September, complementing the vine-shrouded pergola. The spring garden, framed by trimmed box hedges, marks the start of each new year with a fine display of hellebores in March. The final touch to the garden is the superb apple orchard in the finest Norman tradition, with the added twist of a square pond.

We complete our tour of Normandy's gardens in Granville, on the grounds of the Villa Les Rhumbs, which offer a fine view of the Bay of Mont-Saint-Michel and the Channel Islands. This is where the fashion designer Christian Dior spent his childhood. His family originally came from Saint-Sauveur-le-Vicomte, but moved to this splendid villa in 1905. Dior's mother redecorated the villa inside and out before turning her attention to the garden, which she re-created as a typical English park. She designed the terrace, the winter garden, and the pergola, and came up with the idea of a path leading down to the beach. The cliff-top garden is enchanting, with secluded groves, rose gardens, patios, and a pond. Since 1997, the house has been a museum devoted to the history of fashion from 1900 to the present.

Top: The tiled barns in the Plume gardens at Auzouville-sur-Ry. The gardens are famous for their collection of grasses. They also have a delightful square pond set within an apple orchard.

Bottom, left, and right: The red and yellow poppies in the Plume gardens.Bottom, center: The hellebores in the François Les Clos garden in Préaux-du-Perche. The garden's five acres (two hectares) are devoted to all kinds of plants, however simple or old fashioned.

Facing page: In the Plume gardens, the box hedges are mixed in with garden flowers and wildflowers, clematis, scented plants and water plants, hardy perennials and old-fashioned roses. The garden is divided into five themes that vary according to the seasons.

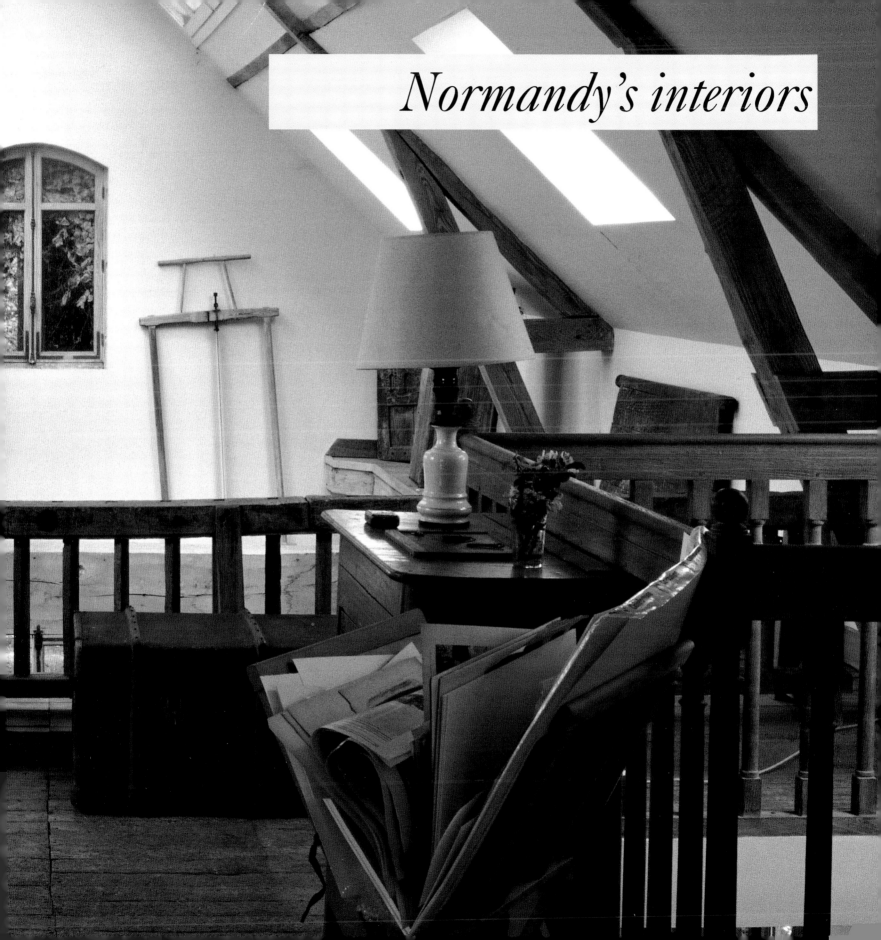

Normandy's interiors

Norman style

E legant seaside villas, Renaissance castles, noble manors, turreted medieval fortresses, half-timbered houses, or simple barns and dwellings once abandoned and now restored to modernity ... whether on the seashore or inland, Norman houses display a huge variety of architectural styles

Besides stately homes, Norman houses, for the most part, take on a humble guise, in tune with their surroundings, the passage of time, and with nature itself. "The castles of princes are made of stone," wrote Patrick Grainville. "The cottage springs from a more popular, familiar mythology.... Hidden away, crouched down, it is a refuge, a sophisticated hut. It is closer to a shelter. A paradise for field mice, muskrats, and spiders.... The mixture of wood, mud, thatch, earth, and clay, imparts a profound truth, and symbolizes mankind in his state of innocence, his infancy. Stone, on the other hand, is already adult."

Since the Middle Ages, the construction of half-timbered houses has continued in its modest way. Almost forgotten during the Renaissance, the technique reemerged at the end of the nineteenth century. It consists of a basic wooden structure composed of vertical posts and interior beams; sometimes an entire tree trunk acts as the keystone for the house. First, the walls are built to provide a foundation and to insulate the house. The spaces between the wooden posts are filled either by rubble stone, a plaster known as "pugging," or a clay-and-straw mortar.

In Normandy, half-timbered cottages often have mullioned windows with window boxes overflowing with geraniums. And the crowning touch is the profusion of flowers—doors are often framed with wisteria and the thatched roofs punctuated by a finial or a row of irises. A garland fashioned of clay and flowers crowns the whole and helps preserve the thatch's moisture. Sometimes, a diagonal bracing or a Saint Andrews cross is added to consolidate the whole, while adding a touch of aesthetic effect to this functional yet pleasing architecture. Roofing, often punctuated by dormer windows, is frequently of slate or tile. Slate, used since Renaissance times, is lighter and more durable than tile and allows rainwater to run off more easily. To highlight this point, some houses in the Auge and in Honfleur have covered even their façades in slate. In the Orne and Calvados, there is a preference for tiles, which are

Above: The Villa Strassburger in Deauville, designed by Pichereau in the early twentieth century. A cacaphony of turrets, balconies, real and faux timber frames. Right: Gentrified outbuildings in Calvados Previous pages: In the Eure, the painter Yuri Kuper's mezzanine.

sometimes embedded in the slate or thatch or placed in a pattern to help create bright spots when reflecting sunlight.

The building techniques used in Norman houses vary throughout the region. At Lyons-la-Forêt, the walls of the houses are made from a *cob*, a mixture of sand, clay, straw, and horsehair or cowhair. In the Caux, imposing farmhouses lie hidden behind two rows of beech trees, earning the epithet *clos-masures*, or closed cottages. In these, the mortar contains pebbles. The basic design, dating from the fifteenth century, is simple, comprising an enclosure surrounded by tall trees, encompassing a dwelling and farm buildings, and afforded a pleasant shade by the surrounding apple trees. Closed off by a large door, the layout is reminiscent of that of a stately home. Inside the grounds, one often finds a pond, a cistern, or a water tower. In the Cotentin, where the weather can be harsh and the sea winds strong, the houses are constructed in groups to offer protection, huddled together to combat the westerly winds and to stay warm. More often than not, these houses are of a single level and are built of sandstone, shale, and granite, with beams fashioned in vertical lines, intertwined, ridged, or undulating like waves. Close to Coutance, the tendency is more toward the white opalescence and bluish hues of the local stone. In the Carentan marshes, cottages with earth-colored walls are the norm.

But whether half-timbered or not, all the houses are the result of an ancestral know-how passed down through generations. Austere on the outside but warm and inviting on the inside, the houses are scattered throughout the Normandy landscape, either sporadically or in happy clusters. From the Swiss Normandy region, famous for its Pont-de-la-Mousse slate in gray-blue and streaked with pink, as far as Cotentin, and from the plains of Caen to the fields of Argentan.

At ground level, the houses in Normandy are mainly floored with flagstones or with variously colored, rectangular, square, or hexagonal tiles in granite, terra-cotta, limestone, or flint. On the upper floors, wood parquet is used. The central staircase forms the center of these houses, with sculpted oak or wrought-iron banisters and steps in elm wood. The character of these Norman houses lies in their mix of wood and terra-cotta—warm and cool materials—and the mineral and earth tones of their interiors. Nearly every room has a fireplace and there are no jarringly bright colors, but rather soothing, pure shades of cream, sky-blue, pale gold, or sea green. The furniture is heavy, almost exclusively in oak, and in the kitchen, copper competes with earthenware and brick. Increasingly, the traditional decoration of Norman houses has been replaced by a lighter and more cross-cultural style, incorporating Scandinavian furniture and flowery, chintz-inspired fabrics.

Above: A typical example of Norman seashore architecture in Houlgate—the balcony of a villa with an awning of sculpted wood and a dormer window.

Facing page: Half-timbered houses—another traditional architectural style in Normandy.

Top, left: Renovated barn in Le Perche. Top, right: Façade of a house with an ivy-covered timber-frame wall in the Plesse. Bottom, right: a thatched house in Saint-Etienne-la-Thillaye, south of Deauville.

Artists' and writers' homes

Their rooms inspire peace and reflection, and are imbued with a delicate, contemplative atmosphere. Despite their very diverse personalities, they all have one unbending rule: simplicity. This can be seen in the materials used, the colors adopted, and the furniture employed—often acquired gradually at antiques shops and markets. This simplicity is also found in the peaceful atmosphere, ideal for relaxation and sharing time with friends and loved ones.

Jacques Prévert's retreat. In 1970 Jacques Prévert and his wife purchased their home in Omonville-la-Petite, on the Channel coast, and moved in the following year. The region was not unknown to the poet, who had been familiar with La Hague since the 1930s. "Fleeing society, Paris life and its literary circles, which had doubtlessly become tiresome for them, the Préverts fell for this part of Normandy," explains Olivia Le Pesteur, who runs the Prévert house museum. The couple retired to this village located in the bottom of a small valley overlooking Saint Martin's cove, twelve miles (twenty kilometers) from Cherbourg. At the far reaches of Cotentin—indeed at the far reaches of the world—they were finally on their own. They loved the place and the simple stone house so much that they continued living there until their deaths in 1977 and were buried in the village cemetery with their daughter. A friend of the couple, Alexandre Trauner, the well-known film set designer (*Hôtel du Nord, Quai des brumes*), was responsible for the house's interior decoration and garden design. He achieved an atmosphere devoid of affectation, meant to promote reflection and serenity.

On the ground floor, the kitchen and the living room floors are covered in *tomettes*, hexagonal-shaped quarry tiles. The first-floor study overlooking the garden is the true soul of the house, with exposed stone work, oak parquet floors, a painted wardrobe, and a squat armchair. Over the fireplace hangs a portrait of the master of the house by Pablo Picasso. The original worktable resting on two trestles is still there, as are the armchairs. For lighting, there are two old enameled lamps. What was formerly the bedroom has been converted into a reading room. Jacques Prévert never really wrote in this room, but he reread manuscripts, corrected

Facing page: In Omonville-la-Petite, Jacques Prévert's house. Roses and other flowers in the garden lend a poetry to the façade of this stone house, with its mullioned windows. Photograph © Maison Jacques Prévert, Conseil général de la Manche. Left: Upstairs, the study's mansarded ceiling and work area, with a simple desktop on trestles surrounded by country chairs placed in front of the window overlooking the garden. Simple enameled workshop lamps light the room.

texts, and made photo collages using photographs by Robert Doisneau and others. Today, the house is a charming little museum with regularly organized exhibitions.

Didier Decoin's house at the head of Cotentin.

From the bedroom windows one sees the sea in all its glory. The writer Didier Decoin and his wife, Chantal, bought the house in the 1980s. It is a small tumbledown cottage at the foot of the cliff at La Hague, near Cherbourg, an optimal position to view the raging sea on a stormy day. "My husband came here to interview Yves Montand and Joseph Losey for the film *Les Routes du Sud*," recounts Chantal Decoin, "and when I came back with him, I immediately fell in love with the place. It has something of Ireland about it." The property that the couple finally bought actually consists of two small fisherman's cottages that the former owner found difficult to part with, but she was happy to pass on something of the happiness she had known there. "And her message got through," confirms Chantal Decoin. "It is a house that is always full, and always very happy. Our children love to come here with their friends, and that's a good sign. It's a real holiday house. All the more so in that we already live in the countryside, so this really rather small house suits us perfectly. We wanted to respect the spirit of the original building, and to create an everyday harmony using simple things." Inside, a combination of three colors reigns throughout the house. Milky walls, gray-blue woodwork—a color also found in the magnificent shale chimney—and a warm beige on the sandstone floors. "We organized our interior around these three colors," explains Chantal. "All of our objects and furniture were acquired from antique fairs and shops, and lots of pine furniture from various periods, as well as a multitude of objects linked to the sea, since my husband adores boats. As for me, I do a little painting, a lot of biking, and, above all, I look after the garden."

Roger Martin du Gard, friend of Perche.

Gone are the glory days of the Château du Tertre, situated in the commune of Sérigny, close to Bellême, in the Orne. Since his death in 1958, everything has remained as it was, or as close as possible to it, since the present-day owner, Anne-Véronique de Coppet, granddaughter of Roger Martin du Gard, the former owner of the estate, keeps his memory alive with a loyal respect for the past. Nothing has really changed, right down to the bouquets of fresh flowers regularly placed throughout the rooms. The office, the most personal of all the writer's rooms, sports a bronze chandelier. A range of ochers and orange tones were employed to coordinate the shades of the divan, the

Roger Martin du Gard purchased the Château du Tertre in 1924 and made this elegant Louis XIII property his principal abode. Using brick and slate, it was built in the great classical tradition with two wings in white stone.

velvet armchair, the rug, and the burlap-covered walls. In this somber decor, so suited to quiet contemplation, there remains still today, impeccably lined up above the writing desk, the gallery of black-and-white photographs of his family and friends, and of special occasions together. Among them are portraits of Gide, Gallimard, Jouvet, Mauriac, and Camus, and placed to the left of the writing desk is an effigy of Tolstoy, as though keeping an eye on the writing's progress. A touching and loyal tribute.

Roger Martin du Gard bought the house in 1924 and made this elegant Louis XIII-era property his principal residence. He had known about the property since 1906, as it belonged to the family of his wife, Hélène Foucault. The fact that his wife was fond of the house no doubt influenced his liking for the place. But even before then, Normandy was home to him. Du Gard even made the region the subject of his doctoral thesis, a treatise on the ruins of Jumièges Abbey. The writer had nothing bad to say about this corner of France: "I am once more conquered by the overpowering and bewitching charm of the region," he writes in his journal. "No other place has attracted me to this extent..." Today, a certain grace surrounds this edifice built in the great classical tradition with its two wings in white stone. A worthy formality that fits well with the alternating brick, stone, and slate of the edifice. Two wings were added close to the watchtowers at the beginning of the nineteenth century. The writer was involved in all the plans, both inside and outside the house, the garden, the architecture, and interior decoration. He freed the walls from their bourgeois wall coverings and gave them a classic varnish.

Inside, Roger Martin du Gard turned convention on its head, transforming the dining room into a vast library in the directoire style. The only fanciful whim in this otherwise rigorous decoration is the earthenware stove decorated with statuettes, and surrounded by gray shelves that the writer designed himself.

In the grounds of the property, Roger Martin du Gard, a perfectionist by nature, sought out harmony and classicism. He opened up the grounds' perspective—over twenty acres (eight hectares) in all—and enlarged the view by removing some trees, thus gaining an enhanced view of the forest, and a glimpse of the church tower at Bellême, whose bells toll the hour. He continues to maintain the two pavilions, dating from Napoléon and built at the same time as the park was planted, one of which he called "the philospher." In order to lend a sense of elegy to the whole, he had a statue of Diana the Huntress erected at the end of

Left: Roger Martin du Gard's room. A range of ocher and orange tones is achieved by the coordinated shades of the divan, velvet armchair, the rug, and the burlap-covered walls. Above: The writer's study, with a collection of photographs on the wall; a touching tribute to old friends.

Right: An anteroom in the Château du Tertre, with an alcove armchair upholstered in floral-print fabric. Left: The main library in the house is in directoire style with the exception of its squat armchairs covered in floral chintz.

the main garden path. Roger Martin du Gard was interested in French garden design and constructed a pond in the shape of a shamrock and even designed its irrigation system which crossed the grounds. The Flore fountain which he positioned next to the pond draws its inspiration from the fountains at Marly.

Besides practicing his talent for decoration, he occupied himself making the Château du Tertre (where, incidentally, he wrote his first novel, *Jean Barois* a site devoted to the arts and letters, bringing together the writers and artists of the Décades de Pontigny in Burgundy and the *Nouvelle Revue Française*. Soon it began to attract the upper crust of the day's intelligentsia, including André Gide, to mention but one, who had a house nearby, at Cuverville, where he would read aloud from his manuscripts on the terrace. Speaking about the Château du Tertre—which was open to all those who wished to meet, rest, work, and reflect—one writer said: "My dreams of the future are here … I dream of a hospitality open to all my friends in an unforgettable place such as this." After its glory years, Tertre went through some difficult times. After the war and the death of Hélène in 1949, it was never quite the same again. Rousing itself from its apathy, the house enjoyed a comeback when André Malraux, Albert Camus, and Jean Delay stayed there. Christiane Martin du Gard received visits from the artists Jean Hélion,

Fernand Dubuis and writers including Jean Tardieu, André Frénaud, and Philippe Jacottet from 1960 to her death in 1973. Today the old spirit of the place thrives again: Anne-Veronique de Coppet has revived tradition by opening its doors to the group Amies du Tertre who organize literary events and visits from theater companies and musicians.

The Delerm house, in the Eure. Located

in the center of the village, this simple stone-and-flint farmhouse dates from the beginning of the eighteenth century. At one time, it would have been home to farmers, but it was enlarged during the nineteenth century and acquired new finery, including some Second Empire fireplaces and wainscoting. Although it gained in grandeur, it never rejected its origins or lost its picturesque appeal. This is where the writer Philippe Delerm and his wife, Martine, an author and illustrator, have lived and worked for the last eighteen years, and where their son Vincent wrote his first songs. "I never would have thought that one day I would live in Normandy," says Philippe. "All the more so because I didn't really know the region. But later I fell in love with its maze of small valleys and rivers, and especially this house that I felt had a soul. It is neither a very practical nor a very functional house, but it doesn't matter, we like it here."

Softening the contours of an otherwise austere structure are the flowers. A circular flowerbed graces the front doorstep, and behind that lies a symphony of roses, peonies, and wisteria intertwined with Virginia creeper. "I had always thought that gardening would bore me," confides Philippe, "but the opposite is true. That said, it is mostly my wife who looks after it." At the edge of the garden, the barn has been preserved and transformed by Martine and Vincent into a small makeshift theater. This is where sketches and sing-alongs are performed when friends come by to spend the evening. The writer, also a teacher at the secondary school in the neighboring town, puts on plays with his students at the end of every school year. "For us, theater is a passion, but above all it is a real family tradition." Inside, nothing has changed. The house is a succession of little rooms, their doorways worn with age. On the floor are the local *tomettes* or quarry tiles and on the ceiling, wooden beams. We are quick to get the message: there is nothing new here, nothing orderly or purely functional, but rather a friendly hodgepodge and an underlying belief in the art of accumulation. "We are a little like rabbits in a burrow," smiles Philippe. "Here, nothing is smooth, sterile, or straight. There is a lot of English furniture in polished pine, family heirlooms, and pieces picked up at antique shops and flea markets. In other words, there are lots of lopsided legs...." The walls too have a lot to say, loaded as they are with exhibition posters, engravings by Jean-Michel Folon, photographs, small

Right: The living room in Martine and Philippe Delerm's house. A succession of rooms, doorframes worn with age, and wood-beam ceilings. On the floor are the local tomettes or quarry tiles. The wicker armchairs add the flavor of summer holidays. Facing page: Top, right: The charm of the country dining room. Center: the writer's work table. Below: The small theater in brick located in the barn, at the end of the garden. Left: The house and its orchard of fruit trees.

paintings, and reproductions of Scandinavian works by Vilhelm Hammershoi and Carl Larsson, on whom Delerm has written several books. Indeed he is passionate about Scandinavian art. Portraits of women's bodies in the half-light, dark interiors with half-open doors; this art is intimate, austere, mysterious, romantic, and dreamlike, an art rich in symbolism. And all the more interesting because of the link between Scandinavian painting and Impressionism—the two having similar dilemmas and treatments of light.

"Our house is suspended in time," Delerm concludes. "It is a place to rest, to collect oneself, to write and paint. It is a house that adapts to all moods. It is perfectly suited to solitude, but also for being with others. And while it is a place where there is a lot of silence, there is just as much laughter, dancing, and playing."

Above: The wrought-iron veranda, whose windows and shutters were salvaged from neighboring houses.
Right: The bedroom's gray-stained beams, as elsewhere throughout the house.
Facing page: Top right: The brick façade of the barn entrance.
Bottom, right: A casual lunch in the garden.

Yuri Kuper's Normandy Dacha.
It is his native Russia, and time spent in various foreign cities, that has had the most influence on the painter Yuri Kuper's work, in particular, on this house situated in the Eure. In 1980, he discovered Normandy. "I fell in love with the area immediately, its climate, its rain, even its occasional snow." Having decided what it was that attracted him, he bought this barn, lost in the middle of a forest, with its brick façade and garden gone to seed. A main building bearing all the marks of time had been adorned with a veranda, and two small new cottages were added to the property. From neighboring properties he salvaged windows, glazed doors, a staircase, wooden fittings, and structural supports, each charged with its own history and its own era, yet brought resolutely into the present with the new design. It is in this Norman setting that the artist produces most of his work and finds his source of inspiration—for many of the same reasons as painters of the past. Paintings and sculptures in metal and wood line the walls of his home, along with more recent work that includes sculptures and compositions made from salvaged items. Photographic negatives of tulips are housed in wooden frames worn down by the rain. Tables and chairs, beams and trestles are all stained a delicate pearl gray, a reminder of the silvery whitewash used in Renaissance times to make polychromatic paintings appear older. The painter uses this time-honored custom to give soul to both his home and to his paintings. "This place evokes for me the same feelings that I have had in Rome or Venice," he explains. "When one looks at the surface of a table, the façade of a palace, or the contents of a canvas, one is looking at history through the fibers of the wood, the cracks in the varnish, or the daubs of the brush."

Facing page: The entrance hall, designed as a loft. To give maximum light, the floor and walls are painted pearl gray. The stairs leading to the first floor were salvaged from an abandoned house.
Right: Top left: To create an informal, friendly feel, the kitchen opens out onto the rest of the house, while the cupboards and countertop were fashioned out of planks of wood.
Top right: A perfect harmony between the brick and the oak beams highlights the original ambience downstairs, with its view onto the garden. A wooden bench and a simple country-style table suffice to create a summer dining room.
Bottom: On both sides of the console, made from a transformed workbench, hang an array of frames; others on the ground patiently await their destiny.

Châteaux, manors and stables

Upon leaving the coast, as you make your way along a country road or valley, it is frequently possible to glimpse, through a set of elaborate wrought-iron gates, the façade of a château, set amid a splendid private park. Often dating from the Middle Ages, most of these structures were severely damaged or destroyed, only to be rebuilt several centuries later. Despite the vagaries of history, they tended to be decorated in the Italian style. With the Renaissance, austerity was rejected and extravagance became all the rage. Order, pomp, and pageantry gained primacy at the expense of a certain simplicity that had existed hitherto. It was the *Grand Siècle* for houses, or the century for great houses, whichever you prefer. In the Orne, north of Cotentin and Bessin, at the end of the fifteenth century, a series of smaller gothic manor houses began to appear next to these imposing country seats. Half-timbered, sectioned, or more prosaically fitted in brick or stone, these multistory houses come complete with turrets, moats, and battlements. Inside is like something out of King Arthur's Camelot. Along with these majestic houses, so evocative of bygone times, it is also worth visiting some of the architectural follies of the region.

At the time it was built, La Maison du Bois des Moutiers, situated on a promontory on the cliffs at Varengeville, about four miles (seven kilometers) from Deauville, was in the vanguard of the Arts and Crafts movement. At that time, the town was very much in vogue, and while less chic than the coastal resorts next door, it was considered to have more gravitas. Designed by Sir Edwin Landseer Lutyens and built in 1898, La Maison du Bois des Moutiers is a blend of the different influences in vogue at the end of the nineteenth century. A turning point in more ways than one, the period saw an interest in ideas as diverse as orientalism, Art Nouveau, naturalism. and the emergence of new spiritual, not to say mystical, movements. At Bois des Moutiers all of these influences are evident. Guillaume Mallet, a protestant and former cavalry officer, purchased the site at the end of the nineteenth century. Intrigued by English gardens, he saw in this site the means to achieve his aspiration of building a house and garden that corresponded to his naturalistic sensibilities and symbolist leanings. His family and friends supported him in his endeavor: first his wife, a Theosophist; then Emily Lutyens, the architect's wife; and finally the landscape designer Gertrude Jekyll, who designed the garden. Edwyn Lutyens went on to design the pavilions at the Universal Expositions in Paris (1900) and Rome (1911) as well as the viceroy's palace in New Delhi,

Above: One of the façades of Bois des Moutiers, with a diagonal exterior staircase that leads to the garden.
Right: The house with its pagoda roofs, stone walls, wood, and brick, and circular or rectangular windows.

Left: The main reception room at Bois des Moutiers. The house features refined furniture, minimalist setting, lead lattice-work windows with unusual closures, and oak shutters and is often the setting for public concerts.
Right: Top: The windows are as narrow and high as those of a fortress or a convent. Bottom: One of the drawing rooms of the house with mullioned windows. The graphic lines of the furniture shows the influence of the Arts and Crafts movement.

and the fountains in Trafalgar Square. In designing this house, Lutyens aimed to reflect both the new ideas of the time and the whimsical flavor that was beginning to be felt along this stretch of the Normandy coast.

Founded by William Morris, the Arts and Crafts movement was in its infancy when Lutyens designed the house, and it became one of the first in France to incorporate elements of this nascent style. The neo-Tudor style at Moutiers is inspired by the work of Norman Shaw, Stevenson, Dovey, and Philip Webb, who in turn was a keen follower of the neo-Gothic movement. Here, everything is crafted with the constant quest to create a meaningful relationship between the individual and his environment. Architecture and decoration come together here in a combination that evokes the kind of gallantries found in romance literature and tales of knights in shining armor. For this, his first private commission, Edwyn Lutyens brought architecture and landscaping together to produce a whole greater than the sum of its parts. He also designed the furniture, which was manufactured by Morris & Company in their workshops at Merton Abbey, and he imported the woodwork, doors, windows, and chimneys from England.

A labor of love. When a young farmer named Michèle Lefol came across the Château de Crossville-sur-Douve in the Cotentin, on the Channel coast between Saint-Sauveur-le-Vicomte and Picaville, she instantly fell in love. The building was in a serious state of disrepair, looking out over a patchwork of fields and marshes. But she was undaunted, and set about saving it. Classified as a historic monument in 1972, the first stones of the house were laid in 1630 by Jean V de Crossville, Lord Chamberlain of the Grand Condé. The overall style remains medieval, with its carriage gate dating from the sixteenth century, its closed courtyard, and bartizan staircase that leads to the upper floors, and the donjon, complete with machicolations.

The fortress had long ago lost the pomp and splendor associated with a manor house and was used only as agricultural buildings. Farming families had lived in the castle itself—one of which were the Lefols, dairy farmers for many generations. As a child, Michèle had played in the castle ruins; as a teenager, she organized visits and dreamed of living there herself one day. When it finally came on the market, in 1980, she borrowed all the funds she could and managed to buy it. The task facing her was enormous: the roof was in ruins, the staircase had been severely damaged during World War II, and the painted ceilings had collapsed. But the house was still beautiful, and her passion for it too strong to be deterred by such details. After mustering up all the grants and loans she could find, she

Left: Detail of a decorated door, in the Château of Crosville-sur-Douve, on the theme of Ovid's Metamorphoses. *Facing page: The castle's formal drawing room is full of architectural and decorative treasures. A decorated floor and a magnificent ceiling, whose multicolored beams are decorated with painted garlands. An exquisite example of seventeenth-century splendor hidden deep within the Normandy countryside.*

founded an association to support her and organized visits, events, and craft workshops. Finally she was able to start renovations. In the end, she was awarded first prize in the Old French Houses competition, and second prize in the Masterpieces in Danger category. Although recognized by several foundations, success has in no way gone to her head; she has her feet firmly on the ground, continuing to run the family farm at the same time as her other projects.

In the Orne, Béatrice and Thierry Ardisson's ark.

This elegant stud farm, dating from the period of Charles X, was purchased by Béatrice and Thierry Ardisson. It had probably once been a residence for one of the king's mistresses, who would have been surrounded here by a peaceful twenty-acre (eight hectare) parkland, exhibiting an astonishing variety of flora and fauna. The English garden is often veiled with a diaphanous, dreamlike haze in the morning. Fortunately, the lime blossoms, maples, and century old trees that toppled over during a massive windstorm that hit the area, in the late 1990s, were all saved, except for one umbrella pine that could not withstand the damage. The garden is overflowing with Pierre de Ronsard rose bushes, and the vegetable garden, surrounded by box trees, is meticulously cared

for by its new proprietors. Palm trees are due to be added shortly, and are bound to add a touch of exotica to the garden.

In the entrance hall, Grandmother's portrait greets visitors and surveys the comings and goings. "At the time, we were looking for a weekend house an hour from Paris," explains Béatrice Ardisson, "all the more so because the children were still small and Thierry's work meant that he needed to be near the capital. We chose this house because it was flooded with light, and we had such a good feeling about it. I discovered afterward that the former owner knew my parents. We became friends, and although she is no longer alive she was immensely important to us when we moved in. We even have some of the furniture that was left with her only to find itself back here later on! Such is life. Nonetheless, the works took twelve years and we are still not finished." Some windows were reopened and most do not have curtains, or at best have Venetian blinds to let the light filter in and reflect the changes in color in the surrounding garden. Decorative elements from former times were also salvaged to add to the feeling of times past, while studiously avoiding clichés. Lighting is an essential component in achieving the overall effect. Lamps are on dimmers, candles abound, and antique enamel stoves are strategically placed for gathering around on winter nights. Another feature of the house is the outbuildings, converted to garages for the owner's collection of cars. "It's a family house that has been reworked to suit our requirements," concludes Béatrice. "I have found here the charm and style of the houses I knew as a child. Our way

Left: The Sai stud farm, home of Béatrice and Thierry Ardisson. Chickens, birds, dogs, cats, and ponies are all part of the menagerie that roams freely about the grounds.
Above: The staircase of the house is a play on stripes and symmetry. A saddle hangs over the banister, a reminder of the original theme of the house.

Here, Béatrice Ardisson created everything with the help of decorator Bruno Desjuzeur, who advised her on fabric and wallpaper. The dominant color is green, for its British flavor. One golden rule: nobility allied with poetry.

Facing page: Top left: A Venetian chandelier hangs under the glass ceiling, forming the center of this brilliant room and suffuses the ceiling with crystalline light. Bottom left: Decorated floors and Empire furniture set the tone for the vestibules, with their exquisite views.

Left: The dining room mixes English furniture with directoire-style pieces, to which are added family souvenirs and religious effigies.

Right: Top: The ultimate in elegance: a marble bathtub matches the marquetry parquet. Bottom: Detail of a bedroom with fabrics from Osborne & Little.

*Left: The library at
Béatrice and Thierry
Ardisson's home. The
ground floor has a
very cozy, British-
inspired ambience.
In order to maximize
the light in each room
there are no curtains
at the windows.
Right: Top: A family
portrait in watercolor,
dating from the start
of the century, and
delightful bouquets of
freshly cut garden
flowers. Bottom:
Resting on a leather
club chair, between
two kilim cushions,
nestles the Persian cat,
one of the many four-
legged inhabitants of
the house.*

Above: A timber-frame house, typical of the architecture around Deauville. Right: The drawing room is a mix of eighteenth-century furniture in dark wood, equestrian drawings by Jean-Louis Sauvat, bright fabrics by Rubelli and Canovas. The interior displays the memories of many voyages.

of living has changed also, since I now live here all year round. Our children go to the local school and it is a great chance for them to grow up in the country. Here you have a real feeling for the seasons, you are nearer to what really matters. And Thierry comes down every weekend."

A renovated stud farm Near Deauville.

This half-timbered two-story house in Deauville, originally dates from the thirteenth century. Since then, it was burned down and rebuilt. A characteristically Norman mix of slate and tile roof, it has two lateral brick pavilions. "I have always lived in Normandy," says the owner, "and my husband and I wanted our children to have the same experiences growing up that we had. A successful house is one where you feel welcome, where you feel at home. No doubt I inherited these ideas from my own family. In our house, Sunday lunch was always a grand affair. It was a real family home." Inside, the décor reflects the owner's avowed penchant for adventurous combinations. Color is paramount: a symphony of green and red in the drawing room, dining room, and library is balanced by white and blue in the bedrooms. The mahogany furniture blends well with contemporary paintings and painted furniture. Items picked up from travels abroad—particularly in Ireland and England—abound, but also pieces found near home, especially at the boutique in Deauville run by Béatrice Augié, who shares her eclectic taste. Everywhere there are trophies, paintings, interesting objects, and memorabilia on the theme of horses and hunting. "Even though we go most place by bicycle, horse riding is an integral part of family life," she says. The soul of a place comes from the artful mixing of valuable items with those of little material value. "Of course we have kept furniture that was in the family, but comfort and coziness are primary." All around the house, nature reigns; ducks and chickens wander freely. In the vegetable garden, the lady of the house finds another outlet to express her taste for unusual combinations, with flowers alongside vegetables, and cows and horses wandering in the meadows and pastures.

Castle life as lived in seventeenth-century outbuildings

First, there is the parkland and the three hundred-year-old trees that give this property its unmistakable character. Then, the outbuildings, nowadays transformed into dwellings, with tiny windows and old-fashioned curtains. Three separate residences were built on this site, and as each one was destroyed, a new one would rise in its place, but not for long.

Above: The outbuildings of the former Château de Manerbe. Inside, comfort and simplicity reign.
Right: The two wings, in brick and stone, built around a pond have an upper floor with dormer windows and a tiled roof.

The first castle, in stone and brick, dates from the twelfth century. After falling prey to the ravages of time, the castle was replaced by a classic seventeenth-century mansion, which proved no match for the upheavals of the French Revolution. After much wrangling, Prince Hanjeri bought the estate and built a château there in the nineteenth century. But unfortunately history was not kind to him either. During World War II, his château fell into the hands of the occupying Nazis, and at the liberation the heir to the estate destroyed everything in an attempt to exorcise it of its inglorious associations. Of the three successive houses, nothing remains but the last vestiges of three epochs of owners, amounting to several outbuilding that the present owner bought a few years ago: two brick-and-stone buildings built around a pond, with an upper story and small dormer windows peeking through the old roof tiles. "We fell for this house immediately because it has all the advantages and none of the inconveniences of a traditional château," says the owner. "We wanted to retain the charm of the courtyard and the buildings while creating a family home for the weekend and for vacations."

The courtyard has a certain roughness about it, with its mix of stone, brick, and gravel, and a central pond where a charming fountain bubbles day and night. In the garden, the opposite effect is achieved, with climbing roses, flower beds, and chevron-shaped brick paths.

Inside the house, two words suffice: comfort and simplicity. "The renovation took two years and was a great experience," says the owner. "We worked with craftsmen who immediately understood what we were trying to achieve here, though we are still not yet finished. We made the downstairs rooms smaller to bring a more human scale and to reduce the distance between the living quarters and the bedrooms." Upstairs, the atmosphere is more traditional; the bedrooms are covered with Jouy fabric. The ground floor has an exotic air about it, as if one had just walked into a safari. The earth-colored floor tiles fit perfectly with the printed fabric wall coverings, designed by Dominic Kieffer, and the delicate floral pattern blends well with the pale beiges and off-white tones of the sofas and Chesterfield furniture. In the dining room, the style is more minimalist, with whitewashed walls, eighteenth-century furniture, a mahogany sideboard and a cylindrical desk.

On the walls, paintings by Antoine Vit, a local painter, and Yves l'Eveque, a landscape painter from Beauce, and sculptures by Prix de Rome prize winners add to the ethereal feeling that permeates the house.

In Le Perche, a monastery is reborn. A chance sighting in a newspaper advertisement—not much more than a postage-stamp-sized photograph—led to love at first sight for this monastery gatehouse located at the bottom of a valley in Le Perche. The site is charged with emotion and feeling. The former owner, an elderly woman, staunchly attached to the past, met with the purchaser, a Parisian with a passion for all things artistic and cultural, and together they hatched a deal. Everything was signed, sealed, and delivered in just eight days. There was just one condition: the property had to be restored to its former glory. Says the new owner, "I first visited it at eight o'clock in the morning, in the rain, in the middle of October. It was neither the ideal weather nor the perfect time to visit, but I was instantly bowled over by it." Of the seventeenth-century stone-and-brick monastery there is nothing left but ruins

From the entrance, the site is extraordinary. Around the lodge are situated the ladies chapel, the former pharmacy, the staff infirmary, the stables, and a saddle workshop since transformed into a library. In the center of all this lies the gatehouse, now converted into living quarters.

The first stones of the monastery were laid in the twelfth century and its fortunes were closely linked to the onslaught of the various religious wars that ravaged Europe. In the seventeenth century it was rebuilt in the baroque style and was completed in 1769, only to be destroyed again during the French Revolution. In the surrounding parkland there remain edifices that testify to the site's past, like the stone fountains, bridges built over imaginary streams, and the moss-covered wooden crosses, a reminder of the mysticism of another era. The entire architectural whole, complete with its ambience of monastic silence, has been restored as promised.

Inside, the house's southerly exposure insures a great abundance of light. The windows are lightly veiled with gauze curtains that match the prevailing color scheme. The pale materials, the staircase, the parquet, and the floor tiles echo the stone walls that are heavily hung with nineteenth-century paintings, including Italian and French still lifes and engravings. The simplest of prints was chosen for the upholstery fabric and, in the first-floor bedrooms, a delicate floral wallpaper.

The library houses hundreds of works of art; the owner finds a refuge and a place to work when he is not in Paris. The furniture—eighteenth and nineteenth-century mahogany—has a style all its own, each piece bought on impulse by the owner.

Despite the otherworldly atmosphere that reigns here—the silence and asceticism of the former order are respected—the owners have made comfort a priority. They have even

Left: Located in the converted attic of the monastery is a vast library containing hundreds of antique and contemporary editions—one of the owner's passions. Facing page: Top: In the parkland, the lawn drapes its emerald cloak under a 600-year old linden tree. Far off, beech and oak trees exhale waves of cool, fresh air. Bottom left: Light-colored materials, parquet, and a marble fireplace in the drawing room echo the stone walls covered in landscapes, French and Italian still lifes and nineteenth-century engravings. Bottom right: One of the monastery bedrooms with a bed in the alcove, exposed beams, and floral wallpaper.

Right: The garden of Laurence Scherrer's home. An ideal lookout for admiring the Seine and the perfect setting for events in the grounds of the property.
Left: The large drawing room, a mix inspired by the Second Empire, where Napoleon III furniture rests side-by-side with memorabilia, antiques, and miscellaneous objects. The walls play host to old portraits and landscapes.

bent the rules slightly, transforming the chapel into a playroom for the children. In the parkland, trees and streams add to the ethereal atmosphere. But, with the exception of a row of flowers around the edges of the house to highlight its foundations, other flowers are limited to a bed of bright daffodils that burst forth in earliest spring followed by scented hyacinths in April.

Magnificent views of the meandering Seine.

Laurence Scherrer's house floats somewhere between heaven and earth, perched on a cliff above La Bouille, overlooking the Seine, on the road to the abbeys of Jumièges and Bec-Hellouin. Country inns, undulating landscapes, and shaded forest paths constitute the principal attractions of this quiet area, situated at the foothills of the wooded valleys of the Roumois plain.

In bygone days, a steamboat would leave from Rouen, stopping nearby where one could try the local specialties of apple turnovers, eel stew with cider, and local cheeses. The site was a favorite with many writers, Hector Malot, for example, wrote *Sans Famille* here in 1878. In Laurence Scherrer's house, everything starts with the blue-gated entrance to the parkland. The house is a former hunting lodge dating from 1878 that Scherrer's father purchased because of the magnificent view. Its roof is in the traditional slate and tile, and the house is surrounded by beech trees, hydrangeas, wisteria, and roses. "It was almost certainly a seafaring family that built this house so they could observe the comings and goings of the ships on the horizon," says the owner. "Originally, everything was rather gloomy here. My mother opened it up to let the light in." In order to make the most of the light, the interior is a kaleidoscope of yellow, red, and green offset by lots of carved wood. The extraordinary kitchen features a bow window, wooden cupboards, and furniture dating from the 1950s that Scherrer has painted bright orange. In summer, five rooms are available to guests for a series of themed literary weekends that culminate, not surprisingly, in one devoted to the area's most famous literary legend, Gustave Flaubert.

Left: In Laurence Scherrer's home the wooden gangway with its colossal vault, like the inverted hull of a ship provides a fascinating center point. The dining room and the billiards room. Right: Animal portraits decorate the walls, in particular cows, in homage to one of Normandy's most important inhabitants, and as a general appreciation of the countryside itself. Facing page: Top right: A view of the first floor, leading to the bedrooms. Bottom right: Detail of a guest bedroom decorated in subtle shades under the eye of an ancestral cardinal.

Family houses

Two styles of building typify the architecture of the Normandy coast. In the Seine-Maritime the tone is more measured than on the Côte Fleurie, which tends to be more grandiloquent. From Dieppe to Le Havre, traditional houses draw their inspiration from those found around Caen, making use of rubble and cut stone and topped off with slate roofs. This is in sharp contrast to the Côte de Nacre where the style prevalent at the end of the nineteenth century tends to dominate. This is where you can see some spectacular villas, with their ornamented façades, highly decorated balconies and balustrades, bow windows, sophisticated roofs, and chimney stacks. Classic villas have no compunction in drawing inspiration from Swiss, Spanish, or even Persian chalets. Traditional local villas use wooden cladding and the villa-chalets combine the two styles. With its diverse range of influences that span from Norman to Alsatian and Scandinavian, the architecture here is not afraid to mix styles in an effort to stand out. As a result, checkerboard façades, dormer windows by the dozen, canopies, balustrades, corbelled features, and finials all make an appearance.

Deauville, where generations come together. Marcelle Barré hales from the Auvergne and her husband, Paul, is from the Loire Atlantique region. Having lived all their lives in Paris, they chose Deauville as the location for their country house. Both were dentists by profession and Paul was to become head of the dental college and, later, a respected local industrialist. Their first house, the Villa Jandy was in Deauville itself, which they sold before moving to Cabourg. Later, they returned to Deauville, this time to the Villa Santa Maria, which was originally a family guest house. "It is the house of my childhood," explains one of their sons. "Now it is a family home; even the garage was converted into living quarters. My mother took care of everything here. She did not change the layout, but she gave the place its soul and made it habitable." With a huge kitchen, bedrooms and dining room, the basement—doubtless formerly used as a pantry and staff quarters, with the service elevator linking the kitchen to the dining room still extant to prove it—has become a very pleasant living area. The living room has elegant bow windows, typical of the region, looking onto the street. While not for a moment ostentatious, the decoration nonetheless reflects a love of the seaside. "The furniture carries memories for all of us," adds one of the owners' daughters. "There is eighteenth- and nineteenth-century furniture that our parents had in Paris. Everything they bought they acquired because they loved it, because it had a connection with a journey or

Left: In Deauville, a villa typical of the region and the town, with two floors, a half-timbered structure, a garden surrounding the house, garden furniture and couch hammock, and a tiled roof. Facing page: In the dining room, the family's furniture reveals a taste for mixed styles and eras. The walls are covered with Canovas wallpaper and decorated with paintings of seascapes, landscapes, animal engravings, humorous paintings, and small portraits. Top right: Detail of a sideboard in front of a painting of antique ruins, a genre popular in the nineteenth century. Bottom right: Detail of a bedroom with eighteenth-century furniture.

someone they met. These are the objects that decorate a life." Upstairs, the rooms have been christened with the names of the colors used to decorate them, so there is for example the blue room and the violet room, some equipped with Portuguese four-poster beds, evidence of the owner's fondness for styles garnered from abroad. The bathrooms also hark back to the past, with double sinks and old-fashioned taps. "Our parents always had a great gift for decorating their homes, wherever they were. My mother has excellent taste and is very knowledgeable. She has a real passion for living and she never veers toward the superficial. She is an extraordinary woman, and loves having people to visit. She is curious and attentive to others, and while she appreciates old-fashioned good manners, she abhors fussiness." The same attention to detail and innate sense of hospitality continues to reign here.

Art Nouveau on the cliffs at Sainte Marguerite.

La Lézardière, in Sainte Marguerite, part of the Caux region, not far from Varengeville, was built in 1903 in the classic Anglo-Norman style. The site is utterly captivating, due to its position on the edge of a cliff, but also because of its location between the Princess Sturdza's gardens and the Bois des Moutiers' parklands. The villas in this lavishly wooded area are said to be among the finest in the region. La Lézadière is one of those seaside villas with an illustrious past. It has been widely photographed, especially on one evening, when Queen Ranavala III of Madagascar dined here, and it has also appeared in numerous books and on postcards. "When we first moved here we felt we were surrounded by spirits and other beings—we thought it was haunted," recalls the present owner, visibly amused by the thought. More prosaically, at the beginning of the nineteenth century, the house had been used as a holiday home for ladies of the night, happy to take the coastal air. Later, the cellist Georges Jean Painvin (who took first prize at the conservatoire in 1901), lived at La Lézardière and would give concerts at the house for family members. But he is above all remembered as a code breaker during the war.

"We came here by chance," say the owners. "With its ocean view, the atmosphere of the house, and the beach, empty from the middle of August on, we fell in love with it straightaway. It is the antithesis of Deauville. We bought it, rolled up our sleeves, and set to work, because everything needed to be redone. The garden was a thicket of brambles, like something out of a Hitchcock movie, all dark and foreboding. We decided to be adventurous in how we used color and opted for pale green in the living room, blood red in the dining room, and yellow for the bedrooms." Inside the house, the ground-floor parquet is in oak and the upper story in pine. The furniture is a mix of styles, genres, and periods, though the overall feel is bohemian. Objects and furniture were salvaged and transformed, so painted chairs turn up in the living rooms and garden furniture sits next to oak sideboards, linking the interior with the exterior. The walls are lined with etchings, drawings, and miniature paintings. The dining room houses a collection of photographs, which the mistress of the house is particularly enthusiastic about; she maintains meticulous albums with snapshots of friends, family,

Above: Brick, cut stone, and a timber frame lend rhythm to the façade of La Lézardière. The house was designed by the architect André Sélonier, taking inspiration from Art Nouveau, the popular movement of the time.
Facing page: Main image: The large dining room and billiards room, with bay window and an impressively high ceiling. Top left: The soft, floral lines find expression in the doors and door handles. Bottom left: A Second Empire sofa combines Venetian and Viennese influences.

Top, left: The façade of Isabelle and Marc Guinoiseau's stone house, with windows composed of six glass panes, typical of houses in the Manche region. A stone path leads to the terrace. Top, right: The bedroom with a wrought-iron bed; a wardrobe in pale pine radiates tranquility. Above: The dining room, with English furniture, bistro chairs, and bookcases. Bathed in a delicate light, it is fashionably simple.

and loved ones who have spent time at the house. "We never wanted to make this place too sophisticated or luxurious," she says. "It is first and foremost a seaside house, and we want it to remain one."

A seafarer's house. Isabelle and Marc Guinoiseau—friends of Martine and Philippe Delerm—have their house at Regnéville-sur-Mer near Coutances, in the Manche. "It was a dependency of the château next door," recount this pair of teachers, "and was fully restored in the nineteenth century. We bought it in 1989 without stopping to think about what we were doing because it was in such bad shape. We started to restore it completely, but were careful to maintain its original features. It is still not completely finished," says Marc, not without a note of pride. This house has an interesting history. A sea captain by the name of Dubreuil, also known as Grand Court, once lived there, and his seafaring obsessions live on to the present day: from every window there is a view to the sea and the bay. Inside, everything is authentic. The woodwork is original and the layout has not been modified. English furniture in pale pine—chosen to blend with the doors—was restored to its original luster and there are books everywhere. "The house is bathed in light," concludes Marc, "and it will outlast us, that much is certain. Even if it does need a huge amount of work, we have the impression that we are doing something good for it, and it returns the favor a hundredfold."

Marie-Pierre Morel's fisherman's house. The photographer Marie-Pierre Morel chose her small house in Agon-Coutainville, next to Coutances, in large part because of the stunning view of the estuary. For someone so professionally concerned with light, location was everything. "But I also like the setting for its inconveniences, for its country feel, its distance from Paris, the bad weather and the isolation, even if the village is a very active little place," says Morel. Just at the entrance, there is a charming little garden filled with flowers and aromatic plants that give off heady fragrances including jasmine, sage, rosemary, thyme, while miniature palm trees add a foreign touch. "I have called the house 'Egg Lodge'," she says, smiling. "It was one of a group of houses centered around a courtyard for fishermen who fished off of the coast of Newfoundland, and I've tried to keep that ocean feel." When it comes to decoration, the tone is low-key. "I drew on the work of the Omega group, founded in 1910, that was based in Charleston, south of London," she replies. "At the time, any surface was considered acceptable for painting on. So I did the same thing here and added little motifs just about everywhere—on the stools and over the chimney for example. I like the slightly New Age feel to the decor, what you could call 'rustic-romantic'."

*Above: The bathroom's
shiny metal tub.
"Everything is a bit
lopsided here,"
explains Marie-Pierre
Morel. "Nothing is in
perfect shape, even the
bathtub leaks a little".
Left: Mix-and-match
is the motto here. The
metal bed becomes a
banquette, the
furniture picked up
here and there has the
patina of age that
confirms its
authenticity.*

Near right, top: The kitchen in Marie-Pierre Morel's house. A larder rests on a painted wooden table, a photograph of Portugal by Jean Dieuzaide. Near right, bottom. The façade of the house in stone and the slate roof. The kitchen is on the ground floor, and the bedroom is on the first floor. Passionate about objects with their own personality and history, Marie-Pierre Morel has found and restored all the furniture in her house herself. The simple furniture was inspired by both the popular arts and the Arts and Crafts movement.
Far right: the kitchen with a cast-iron oven, painted plates, old photographs, and ship's lamp. The seafaring atmosphere is a prevalent theme throughout the house.

In Coutainville, a sailor's weather-beaten cabin. Seven years ago, the journalist Anita Coppet and Jean-Jacques Driewir fell in love with a small nineteenth-century house in the Cotentin, near Coutances, and had to buy it. Made entirely of wood, it is tiny, but rather poetic for that fact, as well as for its mansard roof and bulrush floor coverings. It is a welcoming house, a house for solitude and quiet. "Our first visit took fifteen minutes and all the shutters were closed when we saw it. But we fell for it immediately. We christened it La Hulotte, meaning the Tawny Owl." In former times the sea would have been visible from every window, and while this has changed slightly, the views are still spectacular. The front garden includes tamarisks, rosebushes, arums, herbs, poppies, and peonies. The back garden, tiny as it is, is in the English style. Inside, everything is in wood. "It was undoubtedly some mad cabinetmaker who built this place," explains Coppet. "You can see it in the hundred-year-old pine cupboards with a sheen all of their own." The decoration is minimal and made up of items picked up from all over. "Here, the decorative devil is in the details, in the choice of fabrics and flowers. There is no question of accumulating too much furniture," concludes Anita Coppet. "The aim is to achieve the sort of old-fashioned charm that you find in an old English cottage."

Above: Anita Coppet and Jean-Jacques Driewir's house. The dining room's wicker armchairs and minimalist décor. Above, left: In the bedroom, the wardrobe doors come from Norman wardrobes dating from the seventeenth century that were reused here. "Sometimes it feels like we are living in a ship's cabin," says Anita. Facing page: The kitchen's wooden walls and ceiling.

Contemporary houses

Above: An architect's residence in the Pays d'Auge: an octagonal tower covered in wooden tiles and a huge bay window.
Facing page: Left: View from the living room, with its high ceiling, tall bookcases and Scandinavian influenced functional furniture. On the wall, a cubist-style fresco by the owner's daughter. Right: View of the staircase and dining room furnished in 1950's style; on the wall, an oriental-inspired canvas.

It may not abound with them, but Normandy does have its share of contemporary houses, proud to stand up and be counted as modern, even if they do fly in the face of the dominant style. Unsurprisingly, they are often architects' residences that pay homage to the surrounding landscape, while also blending into it. Lost in nature, they follow the contours of the land and the rhythm of the seasons, the breath and languor of the forests and woodlands. More often than not, they are made from timber, and draw their inspiration from the simplicity prevalent in American and Scandinavian homes. In Normandy, these houses regularly have large bay windows and verandas that open onto nature. Inside, while simplicity may be everything, they are never austere. There is a certain meditative feel to them, with each detail carefully studied in relation to its orientation, and the sources of light and energy. When not handed down from a previous generation, the furniture is often specially designed for the space. The use of wood and a design that is pure and unembellished are in keeping with a philosophy that stresses a return to conservation. Put simply, they emphasize the importance of concentrating only on what is truly essential.

A house in a forest in the Pays d'Auge. Three dates are important in the history of this architect-designed house situated in a glade close to Lisieux, in the Pays d'Auge: 1971, 1981, and 2001. These are the years that two architects, Dennis Robinson and Jean-Pierre Marchand, and an interior designer, Pierre Houssay, used their respective talents to turn a dream into a reality. "More than anything, the house tells the story of a life," say its owners. It was an interesting challenge for the occupants—a historian and an economist—both of who—grew up in eighteenth-century houses, but who opted here for modernism. The idea was simple: a wooden house, opening completely onto nature, with a central building in the shape of an umbrella and a glazed wall all around. The natural order is preserved, and hyacinths, ferns, daffodils, and brooms grow wild. "The forest changes throughout the year. Each season has its tonalities and mysteries, its particular palette of colors. Our favorite season is probably winter, when the tree trunks go from silver-gray to pink-gray. At the end of May begins what we call 'green-hell'." The first part of the house uses a dominant color scheme of golden-beige. "But this has not precluded our adding a touch of fantasy," says the owner. "It has been livened up with spots of red, blue, and ocher, and by frescos that our daughter produced for the bedroom and living room." The furniture was designed for the house and is proportioned accordingly, particularly in the living room where the ceiling is fifteen feet high.

Right: The sunroom of Jean-Loup Eve's house is a focal point of the house. It resembles a glass house flooded with light. With a southern exposure, it has become a warm, sunny living room in its own right. The intricate oriental-style chairs are well matched with the minimalist pine tables.

Facing page: Top: The house draws its inspiration from traditional agricultural buildings, but also incorporates a glass roof. The rose garden and orchard have a vegetable patch and a space for exotic plants. Bottom: A view from the living room of the staircase and the Bauhaus-style fireplace—the long graphic lines magnify the light-filled perspectives.

The décor, too, plays on transparency, combining Scandinavian and Californian influences in simple furniture made of wood and metal. Only the family portraits acknowledge the existence of a past. The kitchen is, of course, used to cook meals, but it also serves as a workshop, sewing-room, and drawing studio if need be. Upstairs, the library contains 2,500 books that seem almost to be hanging from the trees all around. Like a sort of octagonal glass and ivory tower, the house successfully combines both the practical and the leisurely. The eight rooms resemble eight cells, stripped to their bare essentials so as to let the surrounding nature work its magic.

Near Saint-Lô, a sunroom as the center of the house.

The architect Jean-Loup Eve and his wife live in an unusual house, built twenty-five years ago in the middle of a copse, near Saint-Lô. Open to nature, it incorporates silvery green northern pine, brick, and other natural materials.

The house is based upon four open-plan levels and is intimately connected with the natural contours of the site. The overall structure resembles a barn or a traditional farm building. "Everybody calls it 'the Cabin'," says Jean-Loup Eve. "The point was to get away from clichés and build something that drew on the natural energy of the area, while making use of salvaged materials. At first, it was like an empty box, a New Age house, although it filled up quickly once our children came along. We were inspired by the timber houses you find in America and Northern Europe, although, it is not so out of place in this part of the Manche, which is known for being a touch exotic at times. The area is close to the sea, so it is used to incorporating foreign influences."

The living room and sunroom are on the first level, and the bedrooms are spread over the remaining floors, with a guest bedroom under the eaves. The floors are in terra-cotta tiles and the walls in pale gray plaster. But the heart of the house is the sunroom, cooled by trade winds in the summer and warmed by a central fireplace in winter.

The décor is simplicity itself. "It is a bit of everything," confesses Jean-Loup Eve's wife, "a mix of objects, all of which have an association with the sea. Souvenirs from our travels, items we have picked up and restored, family furniture, and some Empire pieces, like a Louis XV1 writing desk and some tables and benches that we designed ourselves. There are also a lot of paintings on the walls, large-scale pieces by Dufour and Coppolani that we've mixed with others painted by my husband in his spare time."

Above: Situated on a riverbank, Jérôme Darblay's house and an outbuilding in the traditional Normandy half-timbered style. Right: Inspired by Scandinavian homes found by the water's edge or on the moor, the red wood contrasts with the greenery of the forest.

A valley in Le Perche.

A *valley in Le Perche.* There are houses that affect you in much the same way as meeting someone remarkable: they change your perception of things, your sense of the world, and, in some cases, the course of your life. The timber house that Jérôme Darbaly built for himself in Le Perche was the catalyst that convinced him to change his profession. A well-known Paris-based photographer, who had worked for all the major design magazines—that all changed when he built his house. He liked it so much, he then set about designing and developing timber houses for others. In Normandy, where half timbering, thatch, and stone walls are the order of the day, this was something of a revolution. "At the outset, nobody could understand why we wanted to build this type of building in Normandy," says Darbaly. "For us it was an important choice, not just because it broke with the style and conventions around us, but because it was a way of reconciling the past with the present. There were personal reasons why I chose this too. I come from a family that had a small paper mill in the Jura, and it is only a small step from paper to wood. At the root of everything, though, were my memories of the mountains and of family holidays spent in a wooden bungalow in the Essonne. But there are more contemporary reasons too. Wood is a way of saying something new and original. It is timeless. It is also ecologically sound, environmentally friendly, and fully recyclable. For a long time, my wife and I looked for a site to build a weekend retreat. We found thirty-seven acres (fifteen hectares) in Le Perche, next to a river. The flowing water was an instant attraction, as was the gigantic elm tree that stands in the middle of the park. The site is all the more magnificent because it sits within a maze of valleys, and the nearby forest helps keep it cool."

Here, everything from floor to ceiling required renovation, so much so that the original house was finally demolished. Responsibility for the new house was given to the architect Bertrand Stoll. The principle was simple, like the materials used in its construction. A timber-frame structure and flagstones for the floor. In deference to the surrounding architecture, the roof uses local tiles. But, above all, this house is the result of a fruitful relationship between owners and architect, from which both sides were able to learn. "We were new to this, but his approach attracted us right away," says the owner. "There was a strong connection between us."

The house occupies five half levels that follow the contours of the site. The plan makes clever use of the space and perspective, with a design that facilitates circulation. In homage

to the timber that was used in its construction, it is conceived like a tree: mineral at the base, vegetable at the top. So terra-cotta tiles were used on the ground floor, white plaster walls on the upper levels, and pale wood throughout. For the décor, an evocative chaos reigns; the decorative elements are the product of a variety of inspirations and sources, including souvenirs from many travels. Furniture in elm and oak come from just about everywhere, including central Europe and the United States, as well as locally from Le Perche. A collection of animal heads lines the walls. "They are not there as hunting trophies," says Jérôme, "but to occupy the space with something unexpected, and to remind us that we are surrounded by nature. Above all else, this house is dedicated to friendship, happiness, and well-being." As if to confirm this, the neighboring barn has been converted into a guest cottage. It is a subject that Darbaly knows well, since, in his previous incarnation as a photographer, he collaborated on a book called "Family Homes."

Above: Right: The huge living room with armchairs and family-sized sofas covered in checkered and striped fabrics. A wooden canoe suspended from the ceiling is a reminder of a journey through Canada. Left: The door that separates the kitchen from the dining room is a remarkable feat of carpentry. Facing page: Top left: A theatrical atmosphere in one of the children's rooms, with built-in painted wooden bed. Bottom left: The bedroom has an old-fashioned bathtub crowned with a baldachin in place of a shower curtain. Right: The wooden staircase affords a spectacular view of the living room. On the wall, hunting trophies are a reminder that nature is everywhere.

Normandy's secret treasures

Rooms with a view

*Preceding spread: The Champ Versan Manor House
in the Pays d'Auge with its two guest rooms.
Above: Two distinct styles of façade on Normandy's
luxury hotels. On the left, the entrance to the
Normandy Hotel in Deauville: verdigris-tinted
and half-timberd, with slate roofs. On the right,
the Grand Hôtel's neoclassical façade in
white stone, which graces Cabourg's oceanfront.*

We begin our tour with the Grand Hotels, with their gilding and pomp, their manners and customs, their nostalgia for past glories, and their continuous renovations. In Normandy, there are three legendary establishments truly deserving of the term "luxury hotel": the Normandy and Royal Hotels in Deauville—two brilliant stars in the Lucien Barrière constellation—and the Grand Hôtel Cabourg. Each of these fine examples of Normandy's golden age continues to flourish along that stretch of coastline known as the Côte Fleurie. But along with these sometimes inaccessible splendors are a range of smaller country hotels and an increasing number of guest houses perched along the sea cliffs and riverbanks, or nestled within fields and forests.

Mythical hotels

Behind wooden façades and pinnacles, painted half-timbered walls and moss-covered roof tiles, the Normandy Hotel exudes an atmosphere that is pure Belle Époque. Facing the sea, it is linked to a casino by an underground passage, and to the town by a horse-drawn carriage. The Normandy has been described as "the only villa in the world with 300 rooms." Built by Théo Petit in 1912, it was an instant success. "It reminds one of a traditional Normandy inn," wrote the press at the time, "and hides its ultramodern conveniences behind a façade reminiscent of a Norman chalet." Naturally, it has been renovated since then—the Paris-based interior designer Jacques Garcia has returned it to its former glory, with soft lighting, candelabras, velvet-covered Second Empire furniture, damask fabrics, and real fires crackling in the fireplace, just as they might in a family home. Not far away, the Royal Hotel, with its typically Norman checkerboard façade, also looks out to the sea. Here, Théo Petit chose a more monumental style, with paneled walls, sculpted wood, marble columns topped with Corinthian friezes, and lavishly draped taffeta fabrics, all lit by lavish crystal chandeliers that hang from the ceiling like stalactites. Jacques Garcia has responded to the structure's intrinsic pomp by using printed velvet fabrics in the bedrooms, marble in the bathrooms, and christening each room after a celebrity guest: Elizabeth Taylor, Bette Davis, Cyd Charisse, to name just a few. In Cabourg, the Grand Hôtel is slightly less imposing, despite a splendid lobby and a series of magnificent bay windows that open directly out onto a sandy beach. Focal point for the Romantic Film Festival, the world of arts and letters has

*Left and above:
Marcel Proust's room
at Cabourg's Grand
Hôtel with its 19th
century furniture,
wrought-iron bed,
and chairs covered
in floral fabric.
A simple interior
which contrasts
sharply with the
ornate salons he
frequented in Paris.*

made this hotel its watering hole, no doubt because of its association—albeit apocryphal—with Marcel Proust, whose specter continues to haunt this lovely and vibrant luxury hotel.

Any first trip to the Seine et Marne *départment* must include a stop at the Château de Sassetot, just over a mile inland. Both a hotel and tearoom, it was assured its place in history when Austro-Hungarian Empress Sissi stayed there. The Empress was captivated by the serenity of the Chateau's landscape, the lushness of the surrounding valleys, its proximity to the sea, and the mystery of its forests, which, being a true sportswoman, she avidly explored on horseback. It must have appeared so different from the rocky cavalcades of Bavaria and the complicated splendors of the Austrian court. In 1875, she spent August and September at Sassetot, where she would expertly ride sidesaddle through the twenty-five acre (eleven hectare) park and bathe in the sea at *Petites-Dalles*. Naturally, one of the walkways in the park has been given the sobriquet "Imperial" to commemorate her visit.

Not far from Honfleur, the Ferme Saint-Siméon is a reminder of the area's artistic associations. Camille Pissaro gave a simple description of this establishment that dominates the Seine estuary: "A farm surrounded by apple trees planted in meadows overlooking the sea…." Penniless painters such as Eugène Boudin, Claude Monet, Alfred Sisley, Gustave Courbet, and Johan Jongkind, entranced by the light to be found at the estuary, would often stay here. The proprietor, Madame Toutain, made them welcome and was happy to accept a painting in payment. The fruit of these exchanges still decorates the walls of what has since become a luxury country-house hotel. Times have changed, and the bohemian ambience that once reigned here is gone. Camille

Above: Left: The Hôtel de Sassetot in the Seine-Maritime was made famous by the Empress Sissi of Austria, who spent holidays in this seventeenth-century château. Right: The entrance to the dining room with its checkerboard patterned tiles, carved oak doors, and coffered ceiling. The château also houses a gourmet restaurant.
Facing page: Top: Near Honfleur, the garden at the Ferme Saint-Siméon. In earlier times, the proprietor of this inn, Madame Toutain, would welcome penniless painters. Nowadays, it is an elegant country-house hotel. Bottom: The dining-room with half-timbered walls and combinations of printed fabrics.

Corot's studio has lost its mournful grayness and has been transformed into a bedroom decorated with Canevas fabrics. But the menu has remained resolutely Norman: sole in cream sauce, fish soup, crêpes flambéed in Calvados, and hot apple tart all make an appearance. Indelibly marked by its historic past, it has shown itself open to the present, as evidenced by the health-and-fitness center with a décor worthy of a Florentine palace.

The quiet attraction of guest houses

Faithful to all the rules of hospitality, guest houses are a new addition to Normandy's tourist landscape, so much so that there are now more than 350 of these welcoming accommodations, catering to visitors weary of the formulaic uniformity of many traditional hotels. Both parties to this transaction are happy with the outcome: owners are only too pleased to throw open their doors and extend a welcome to visitors keen to experience country living and discover local traditions, manners, food, and lifestyle. Visitors receive a welcome worthy of long-lost friends or relations, and are delighted to spend a few days or a long weekend on a farm or in a country manor at exceptionally reasonable prices. The only drawback is the limited number of rooms, so while the chance to get away from it all is not to be missed, remember to book well in advance.

With a façade that combines wood in the famous checkerboard pattern with brick and local stone, the Champ-Versan Manor in the heart of the Pays d'Auge region of Calvados is firmly rooted in the history and landscape of the area. Because it has only two rooms, one in the main building, the other in the tower, one could be forgiven for not taking it too seriously. But this would be a mistake. Its Renaissance-era décor and the generous hospitality shown to each guest make this a unique lodging indeed. The farm's outbuildings accommodate a bakery, carriage house, cowsheds, a cider press, stable, a distillery for making eau-de-vie, and a laundry. "We have done everything to bring the place back to what it originally was," says the owner, "while keeping things simple and in their proper historical context." The sundial, the two towers, and the wooden entrance door, decorated with sculpted acanthi leaves and latticework, add a sophisticated refinement to an already impressive site. Other notable features of this home are the sumptuous medieval stone fireplaces that had been hidden behind a later series of hearths and were rediscovered by accident in 1979. The same fate awaited a kitchen garden and a period cooking stove that were restored to what must have been their past glory. The rest of the décor is strictly Norman, including a selection of eighteenth-century furniture, a hunting table, an opulent sideboard, lofty fireplaces, and curtains made from fine fabrics that permit the light to gently filter into the rooms.

Left: A dramatically decorated guest room at the Champ-Versan manor with a mediaeval fireplace. Facing page: Main image: The dining room's original tiles and seventeenth-century furniture. Top right: A carved detail from the oak door of a Normandy wardrobe. Wardrobes were often offered as wedding gifts, and the carved flowers and doves used to decorate them were meant to bring good luck. Center and bottom right: A collection of eighteenth- and nineteenth-century pottery from Pré d'Auge and seventeenth-century earthenware tiles. Traditional handcrafts that have since disappeared.

*Left: The salon in the
Milles Feuilles guest
house in Calvados.
An elegant and airy
composition that
combines shades of
ecru with fabrics
subtly faded to achieve
a poetic harmony.
Right: Top left: In the
kitchen, a collection
of metal sieves. Top
right: Earthenware
plates and an
avalanche of crystal
cast a golden glow in
the rooms at night.
Bottom: In the
bedrooms, the charm
of carefully chosen
antiques. The
headboards on
the beds are made
from old wardrobe
doors stripped to
the original wood.*

Above: La Maison de Sophie in Saint-Étienne-la-Thillaye in Calvados is a former priory house now transformed into a guest house where the hostess also gives cooking classes.

Facing page: Main image: In an island of greenery in the north of the Cotentin, the stone façade of the Fossardière hotel and a rustic stream. A former bakery has been converted into a breakfast room. Top right: The fortress at Cap Lévi at the tip of the Cotentin is a former military fortress that was renovated and now welcomes guests. Center right: The breakfast room offers a spectacular view over the sea. Bottom right: The salon of the Neptune Hotel in Agon-Coutainville again has a stunning view especially at high tide.

South of Lisieux, in Cerqueux near Orbec, is the Manoir des Mille Feuilles, a nineteenth-century country home, where each room is named after a variety of tree. Its pink pebble-dashed walls and century-old trees envelop a dwelling that houses 1940s porcelain, crystal glasses laid out on linen tablecloths, candlelit rooms, and bedroom furniture, whose luster is evidence of its opulent past. Pierre Brinon and his business associate Philippe Landri have combined these elements to create an environment that has become legendary in the heart of the Pays d'Auge. The elegance here springs from intelligent combinations and finely chosen details: centerpieces of wild achilleas, Murano glass vases, and a glazed earthenware fountain from Apt. The two creators are no strangers to success when it comes to combining gastronomy with magnificent settings—they once opened a restaurant under the same name in the Marais district of Paris, which has since been transformed into a florist and home-decoration boutique. Their experience has paid off handsomely here in this labyrinth of peaceful rooms, perfumed with bouquets of fresh flowers changed daily, and in the drawing rooms with their welcoming fireplaces.

Another guest house, no less stylish or hospitable, is La Maison de Sophie at Saint-Etienne-la-Thillaye, south of Deauville, which is housed in a former priory where animals now roam freely in the grounds. Sophie Dudemaine is a television chef and author of seven books published by Éditions Minerva on such sweet subjects as cakes, crêpes, jams, and madeleines. With the help of her husband Jacki, she opened this five-room guest house, where each room is carefully decorated. The food is, of course, first-rate, and between meals, or after a siesta and a stroll through the gardens, the hostess gives cooking classes, during which she reveals some of her secrets. Every moment here has its own dose of magic: wake up to the aroma of freshly baked bread and cakes; stroll leisurely through beautiful grounds, and dine by the fireside with a glass of wine, its delicate hues brought to life by the flames leaping in the grate.

The Channel coast generates an altogether different set of emotions—the fort at Cape Lévi, buffeted by waves crashing off the ocean, for example. Just a few miles east of Cherbourg, it was built in 1801 as a coastal protection, standing 115 feet (thirty-five meters) above the sea. Upon decommissioning, it became a guest house, and windows were added to the rear, allowing the light to penetrate its inner reaches and rendering it less austere and fortress-like. Indeed, the only vestige of the past is its drawbridge entrance. The interior has been transformed into a reception suite, an exhibition center, an auditorium for recitals, a theater, and a country guest house, where each one of its few rooms has a breathtaking view. At the far end of the beach that runs below the fort is the Fermanville signal station.

With oak parquet floors, mullioned windows, and delicate pastel-colored moldings, the three guest rooms at the Pont-Rilly manor in the Contentin, nine miles (fifteen kilometers) from Cherbourg, have succeeded in retaining their original character. The same degree of refinement

Left: Top left:
A room at the Pont-Rilly manor, with high ceiling and seventeenth-century furniture. Top right: Detail of a luxurious bathroom with a golden double washbasin. Bottom: The former kitchen is of monastic simplicity, with a stone fireplace and original trammel. It is now used as the guests' breakfast room. Right: The Pont-Rilly manor house, located near Valognes and Cherbourg, is a relatively modest sixteenth-century manor house that was converted into an elegant residence in the eighteenth century.

Right: The Isle Marie Château at Picauville in the Manche. Once a fortress, it has since been transformed into a guest house. Facing page: Main image: The main salon boasts a vaulted roof, original furniture, and walls either paneled or lined with intricately patterned fabric with stylized motifs. Top left: The staircase and carved oak banister in the style of Viollet-le-Duc. Center left: A family portrait above an eighteenth-century sofa. Bottom left: In each guest room, floral-motif are beautifully employed.

is also evident in the bathrooms, where bathtubs and sinks are fitted in white-washed oak. Now a protected monument, the house was originally a rather modest country manor. In 1765, the architect Pierre-Raphaël de Lozon added two pavilions and the main entrance, and with those additions, gave it its glory. Another architect, Nicolas Durand, from Paris, completed the project, including the main courtyard, the chapel, the outbuildings, and the stables. Surrounding the château is a forty-acre (fifteen hectare) park, filled with century-old trees, a series of ponds and a water mill that runs on an ingenious hydraulic system dating from before the revolution.

The Cotentin's mix of coastline and woodlands allows its hotels to blend discreetly into the landscape without interfering with the natural beauty of the countryside. Its long stretches of beach are ideal for relaxing horseback rides, solo or in a group, where one can gallop or trot through the fine sea spray against the backdrop of the setting sun. Several hotels offer the opportunity to savor these pleasures, including the small Hôtel Neptune at Agon-Coutainville, whose balconies overlook the water and, most impressively, the Cotentin headland. Another is the Hôtel de La Fossardière, located in one of Saint-Martin's colorful valleys in Omonville-la-Petite, one of the prettiest villages in La Hague. Here, relaxation is synonymous with well-being, since, in addition to the lovely view from its ten tastefully decorated rooms and its bakery which serves fresh, delicious breakfasts, the hotel has a sauna and baths, and offers a range of hydrotherapy treatments.

At the Château de l'Isle Marie hospitality is the order of the day. The owners, the Count and Countess of La Houssaye, welcome their guests in a large drawing room complete with a stone fireplace and walls hung with family portraits that cast a sharp eye over new generations of guests. The elegantly furnished rooms look out onto the parkland and the marshes beyond. Yet, in the past the house had none of this elegance, having once been a Viking fortress. Over the centuries it shed its warlike aspect and softened its contours. Jean de La Varende wrote of the castle's beauty. The Marshal of Bellefonds added several outbuildings, including a chapel designed by Mansart. While the fortress has a certain majesty about it, it in no way overshadows the outbuildings, which have been converted into delightful guestrooms.

In Nocé, in Le Perche, next to the Lormarin Manor, the Maison du Fournil (the bake house) offers a small apartment complete with a whitewashed living room, period furniture, and an ancient bread oven that is still in use. Stables, bake house, inner courtyard, and outbuildings surround this medieval house built by René de la Bretonnière at the end of the Religious Wars, and renovated in the seventeenth century. In 1668, Philippe Turpin changed the fireplaces, restructured the spaces, and renovated the kitchen. In the outbuildings, the Alban workshop sells arts and crafts, small pieces of furniture, and souvenirs.

The road that leads to the Moulin de La Pleugère cuts across the fields of Perche. Upon leaving the road, a waterfall indicates the proximity of the mill. The guest house has a single 1,000-square-foot (100-square-meter) room in one of the outbuildings, with a view over the

Right: Top left: The ceiling of the library at the Manoir de Lormarin with exposed white beams. Top right: The dining room with a simple oak table and Normandy-style wardrobe with carved doors. Bottom: The façade of the Manoir de Lormarin in Le Perche with two stone towers and outbuildings built c. 1565. Left: In the minimalist guest-bedrooms, the furniture is simplicity itself, a throwback to the charm of simple peasant houses where everything had its place.

Left: At the Moulin de la Pleugère in Le Perche, a guest room under the eaves, together with an open plan bathroom. Facing page: Main image and center right: The salon's chestnut ceiling and terracotta tiled floor, Chesterfield and eclectic furniture styles coordinated by the use of bold colors. Top right: The weather-beaten façade of the Moulin de la Pleugère, a nineteenth-century residence in cut stone that bears the hallmark of time. Bottom right: An antique escritoire desk in oak.

river and the hills, where all the contents are for sale: engravings, ornaments, dressing tables, and armchairs. Further away, a barn houses an antiques shop full of eclectic objects—decorated wooden furniture, model boats, birdcages—the perfect chance to find a souvenir as a reminder of one's stay. The Moulin de la Pleugère itself is an elegant nineteenth-century building shrouded in greenery and surrounded by ten acres (four hectares) of meadows and woods, while just beyond, rivers and mills vie for attention among the rolling hills. Its white and yellow sandstone façade and roof of flat tiles have been completely restored. The entrance is through the kitchen, a former stable that still contains a stone trough. In the ample living room, the décor is mixed: a Chesterfield sofa, an eighteenth-century armchair painted white and covered in taupe velvet, a large fireplace, a polished wooden sideboard, a ceiling with chestnut beams, quarry tiles underfoot, and an elegant staircase salvaged from another house. Everywhere, there are curious objects picked up here and there, a reminder that life is nothing more than a series of meetings, associations, and random occurrences. Curiosities like hedgehog skeletons, stuffed turtledoves, religious statues in plaster, workbenches, antique earthenware, and prayer books deliver their subliminal and mystical messages. Here, everything gives off the air of bygone times, right down to the cast-iron bathtub.

Flavors of Normandy

Above: An apple tart, the epitome of the Normandy dessert, is best sampled with a small glass of cider. Facing page: The covered food market at Dives-sur-Mer dates from the fourteenth century and has a magnificent timber framework, a masterpiece sculpted by craftsmen in the Middle Ages. The market is at its finest on Saturday mornings, when the best regional produce is sold.

The Norman's legendary hospitality, penchant for the outdoors, common sense, and love of the good things in life are just a few of the elements that make Normandy so attractive. The region is rich in local specialties, especially when it comes to matters gastronomic—the warm aroma of a caramelized apple tart, pancakes stuffed with wild mushrooms and crème fraîche (the thick sour cream found everywhere in the region), the many renowned cheeses, jugs of fresh full-cream milk, bowls of cider, and the homemade Calvados, guaranteed to bring a warm glow. The cultural importance of food and its ability to bring people together are well known. When one eats in Normandy, the moment is indelibly etched onto the deepest recesses of one's gastronomic memory only to be brought instantly to the surface at the merest thought of the area.

In this part of France, eating is a sacred ritual. Although not the best cuisine for keeping trim, in a region where extravagance and the label "full-cream milk" are signs of epicurean refinement, this is not to be expected. A common theme, or rather a common pair of ingredients, are crème fraîche and apples. A tradition handed down from generation to generation, these two items crop up again and again. Montaigne said of Normandy that it was the region where eating was a science, and that eating well here goes without saying. In France, the names of dishes from Normandy, often incorporating a reference to the area it comes from, are synonymous with great cuisine: leg of lamb from the salt marshes of the Cotentin; *andouille de Vire*, the cured chitterling sausage from Vire; tripe cooked in the style of Caen; and of course stewed pears with sweet cider.

Our gastronomic stroll starts with the spectacular selection of local specialties in the covered market at Dives-sur-Mer on a Saturday morning. In addition to the magnificent half-timbered houses typical of the Auge region of Normandy, the market in Dives-sur-Mer, with its mixture of clay and straw that fill the spaces between the columns of its wooden frame, is a wonderful example of the town's architectural style. It is one hundred feet (thirty-two meters) long and thirty-five feet (eleven meters) wide, with an old cider press that nowadays acts as a pillar and an old flagstone floor. To reduce drafts, one of the original walls was filled in, and to let the light in, three skylights were added to the roof. Although ancient, the building cannot be said to have suffered too much with time. The main supporting pillar, on the rue Paul-Canta, was erected in the fourteenth century and the second part of the building a century later. In the summer it is an oasis of cool.

After the market, head over to the best restaurant in town, Chez le Bougnat next to the church. Le Bougnat means "the coal man," referring to the tradition whereby coal and drink were sold by the same vendor, and where, in the depths of winter, one could sit around the stove to stay warm. In the 1940s, there was a hardware store on the site, and forty years later Chez le Bougnat opened here. The atmosphere is casual, the food authentic, and the setting, with its jumble of objects garnered from antique fairs and flea markets, picturesque. François Teissonnière's success with this three-part formula is augmented by his use of local ingredients. Here, generosity comes first: the portions are as large as the prices are reasonable.

At Gonneville-la-Mallet in the Seine-Maritime, the Vieux Plats restaurant, run by Lucette Aubourg, is a town legend. Calvados and old lace is the atmosphere here. The walls are decorated with hundreds of porcelain plates, frescos, portraits, and landscapes. Letters from famous people line the window and the guest book is a veritable Who's Who. The kitchen oven is one hundred and fifty years old, and the furniture gives off the mellow scent of polish that one finds in old houses. Guy de Maupassant once enjoyed its reassuringly domestic décor, as did Maurice Leblanc, creator of Arsène Lupin, the gentleman burglar. Victor Hugo, Jean-Paul Sartre, Albert Camus, and, in more recent times, the composer Michel Legrand all enjoyed its hospitality. The restaurant is particularly popular on Wednesdays, after the market.

On the banks of the Orne canal in Benouville is the Café Gondrée, which earned its place in history on June 5, 1944, when this family home became the first to be liberated by the Sixth Airborne Division of the British Army. It is said that the owner promptly cracked open his entire stock of champagne for the troops. In 1990, the original Pegasus Bridge, which abutted the house and joined the two banks of the canal, was replaced, but the house and café remained intact—still in the hands of the same family, and kept just it as it was by Arlette Gondrée. A museum and souvenir shop complete the atmosphere.

In the last twenty years, Normandy has become one of the most important producers of oysters and scallops in France, most of which come from the Cotentin coast, in particular from Saint-Vaast-la-Hougue. But it would be a shame to mention only scallops among the surfeit of seafood available on this coast. Lobster, shrimp, spider-crabs, cockles, mussels, periwinkles, sole, and sea snails from Granville are just some of the other delicacies available, best eaten with rye bread and salted butter and washed down with dry cider.

Situated between Le Havre and Étreat, La Villa, a first-class restaurant with a majestic view of the sea, was once inhabited by Armand Salacrou, a member of the Académie Française. With its characteristic wood and brick façade, typical of coastal houses, La Villa offers a regional menu that depends in large part on what the tide brings in. Oysters and lobster naturally make an appearance, but so do local foods, foie gras, and gourmet dishes like knuckle of veal braised in wine lees.

The heart of Normandy beats somewhere between the sea and the countryside, and while it is justly famed for its seafood, it is equally renowned for the quality of its poultry, game, and wonderfully marbled beef that asks nothing more than to be fried in butter.

Above: The Café Gondrée on the banks of the Orne canal, complete with flags and its own miniature museum. It earned its place in history as the first house to be liberated at the end of World War II. Facing page: The restaurant, Chez le Bougnat, at Dives-sur-Mer, is a former hardware store. It is renowned for its regional cuisine, as well as its décor, concocted from every source imaginable. The storefront resembles an antiques shop and the staircase is crowned with an old model airplane.

Above, top: Founded in 1835, the Vieux Plats restaurant is a veritable institution with its pebble-dashed façade decorated with two medallions surrounded by scallop shells. Center: The kitchen's old ovens. Bottom and right: The dining room, decorated with earthenware dishes, frescos, portraits, landscapes, and antique glasses.

Below: The half-timbered façade and thatched roof of the Auberge des Deux Tonneaux in Pierrefitte-en-Auge. A former residence dating from the seventeenth century, it now specializes in regional products and has a large selection of Pommeau *and* Calvados. *Bottom: The restaurant's wood-beam partitions and rustic tables set with white linen, or sometimes with oilcloth—traditional décor to match a menu conceived with a nod to the past.*

Right, top: The restaurant at La Cale in Blainville may be sparse, but its décor—including wooden benches and long tables—is playful. Right, bottom: The sun-drenched terrace of the Auberge de Goury at Cap de la Hague. Facing page: Turn-of-the-century furniture in the dining room at the Grandes Marques restaurant in Saint Pierre-l'Église. Thonet chairs and wallpaper. Facing page: Top left: In Beuvron-en-Auge, the Café du Coiffeur's half-timbered façade. Center left: A table and a bottle of cider at the Bouche à l'Oreille café at Beaumont-le-Roger in the Eure region. Bottom left: The Un Jour d'Éte tea-room in Veules-les-Roses. A tastefully restored house, the awnings decorated in latticed woodwork.

Other specialties include black pudding and *andouillette*, fresh chitterling sausage from Montagne-au-Perche and Mornay, and pan-fried veal chops flambéed in calvados and finished with cream. Turkey, chicken, and rabbit are often cooked according to the Auge Valley recipe that includes a garnish of baby onions, crème fraîche, flambéed calvados, and cider; while Cotentin-style chicken is wrapped in buttered paper and pot roasted; and *pommes à la grivette* potatoes baked in buttermilk and sugar.

The bells at the tiny church situated next to the Deux Tonneaux ring out to announce matins, the Angelus, and vespers. Life here is as simple as the food at the inn: free-range chickens, tripe, crêpes, fried eggs, apple tart, cider from the barrel, and farmhouse calvados. Enjoy these traditional dishes either in the courtyard among blossoming apple trees and magnificent views over the Touques valley, or at a long country-style table in the restaurant's main dining room. Eating well is the priority at this half-timbered, thatch-roofed seventeenth-century inn, typical of the Auge region. Everything here comes from the local hen house, fields, and orchards. Inside, the bar is made from a three-hundred-year-old tree trunk supported by a cider barrel at either end. The décor makes no concessions to modernity, opting for red-and-white checkered curtains, oilcloth-covered tables, wooden joists, and copper pots.

Its stone and red pebble-dashed façade clashes just a little with those of its neighbors, but the *Grandes Marques* bistro, founded in 1920, has always been a bit of a curiosity in the village of Saint Pierre-l'Eglise, on the Manche coast. This family "pub," with a dark, wood-paneled interior, has a certain British feel to it. "Here, everything is homemade," confirms Sylvie Warlop, "in the old-fashioned way. *Andouillette* is our specialty, but we also have fresh bacon, desserts, and once a fortnight, paella and couscous."

In Veules-les-Roses, some of the old fishermen's homes have been transformed into tearooms. Adorned with a decorated timber frame dating from the beginning of the century, Un Jour d'Été has been recently restored. Club armchairs give it a cozy, British atmosphere and the color scheme—red inside, blue and white outside—and exceptional location in one of the most spectacular areas of the Seine-Maritime, make it an ideal resting spot

If after a walk in the forest at Bellême you feel the need for refreshment, do not miss the chance to have tea at the Maison d'Horbé. Situated in La Perrière, between Mortagne and Mamers in the Orne, tea (almost a high ritual here) is served with toast and homemade jams such as grapefruit, orange, lemon, mango, pineapple, or grape. The host concocts these delicacies himself, and also serves his own cakes and regional specialties, including a delicious foie gras. All of this is served amid the crockery, furniture, and jewelry also for sale here as part of the tearoom's other function as an antiques shop.

Right: Top right: Architectural detail from a house in Louviers in the Eure region. Top left: The dining room at Susan Herrmann Loomis's guest house, where lunches prepared in her famous cooking school are served. Bottom: A summer table in Susan Loomis's garden. This Englishwoman, passionate about French cooking, has found in Normandy the sort of easy living one also can also enjoy in the English countryside.

Left: The antiques corner of the Maison d'Horbé in La Perrière, with old-fashioned crockery, silverware, and glassware. It is the most fashionable tearoom, antiques shop, and literary café in Perche. Facing page far top and bottom: Shortbread cookies in old glass cloches, and homemade jams served in silver-plated dishes at the Maison d'Horbé.

182

Dairy products form the basis of much of the region's traditional cuisine, and their quality is due in large part to the quality of the livestock. The resulting comestibles—often using butter and crème fraîche—are exported worldwide, although the emphasis on healthy eating has meant that sterilization and reduced-fat products are increasingly common. Dating from the seventeenth century, the famous Isigny butter is manufactured in the Bay of Veys. Its subtle taste, due in part to its proximity to the sea and ports, has made it popular around the world, and it can now be found in England, the United States, and the Netherlands.

Crème Fraîche is an integral part of Normandy's culinary tradition. It is the elixir that graces all those treasured recipes handed down from generation to generation. With its mellow ivory color and rich flavor, it is the perfect companion for meat, fish, vegetables, and even game. So much so that it has become a synonym for sauce. Combined with white wine, it becomes the perfect accompaniment for the sole served in restaurants from Tréport to Cabourg. Sole Normande, cooked with mussels, oysters, and mushrooms, and combined with prawns, deep-fried gudgeon, or smelt and crayfish cooked in court bouillon, was invented in the nineteenth century by the chef at the restaurant Rocher de Cancale in Paris. Although restaurants in Normandy may be keen on meat and the liberal use of crème fraîche, the region's only organic restaurant is an exception to the rule. Formerly a manor house in Lisieux, the Salamandre restaurant, in Étretat, was rebuilt in the half-timbered style typical of the region, with a design conceived by an architect by the name of Mauge, who was an early fan of recycling and built the house entirely from salvaged material.

Few gourmands would disagree that no meal is complete without a cheese platter. And obligatory on any good cheese platter is Camembert. Though now considered legendary, this cheese, with its soft interior and bloomy rind, only became popular in the nineteenth century. Camembert originated in Vimoutiers, and in the village of Camembert in the Pays d'Auge, and owes its success to Marie Harel, a rosy cheeked Normandy girl who was born in the village of Beaumoncel in the seventeenth century. The recipe is timeless and cannot be tampered with. The key ingredient is the finest Normandy *lait cru*, full-cream, unpasteurized milk heated to just about body temperature. A series of steps, with terms that evoke a scientific experiment, then take place: curdling, slicing, molding, unmolding, drying, and salting using a penicillin-based ferment. Finally, the cheese is left to rest in huge drying rooms where the precious mold is allowed to develop and then, in a part of the ritual that is absolutely paramount, it is carefully packaged in beautifully wrapped wooden boxes.

Besides Camembert, Normandy has a wide variety of other cheeses. Pont l'Eveque is another soft cheese with a moldy rind that dates from the thirteenth century, and Livarot,

Above: The Salamandre is the only organic restaurant in Normandy. The medieval house was originally in Lisieux, only to be dismantled and rebuilt in Étretat. The restaurant wages war on traditional Norman recipes that make liberal use of cream and butter.

Above: A meringue with whipped cream at Gérard Lecoeur's pâtisserie—a speciality served only on Sundays.
Left: Gérard Lecoeur's patisserie in Étretat, founded in 1845 and famous for its ethereal pastries, cakes and candies. A stop here is a must if you are in town. The patisserie also serves as a tearoom with unforgettable lemon tarts.

a comparative youngster at only three hundred years old, comes from the village of that name in the Pays d'Auge. Produced since the eleventh century in the region of Bray, Neufchâtel is a cow's-milk cheese recognizable by its white rind dotted with red and its pale yellow inside. It is the doyen of Normandy's farmhouse cheeses and is nowadays available in various shapes and sizes, including cylindrical, square, briquette, and heart-shaped. Full-cream butter is used in the light, flaky Norman pastries and gives character to the infamous brioches, puff pastry, and apple turnovers, and mini-brioches known as *fouaces* or *falues*, along with a host of other heavenly delights.

If you have a sweet tooth, do not miss Gérard Lecoeur's pastry shop in Étretat, which dates from 1845. Besides his toffees, the shop is renowned for its cakes, with emblematic appellations in tribute to the celebrities of the day. In homage to Offenbach's *Vie Parisienne*, the Brésilien cake is named after the composer, while the Rayon Vert is named after Jules Verne, and the Marguerite after Mme Maurice Leblanc. It is said that her husband wrote his novel *L'Aiguile Creuse* while enjoying pastries flavored with almond and orange-flower water.

The Maison du Biscuit, in Barneville-Carteret on the coast of the Manche region, is another magical spot for pastry lovers. This family business is run by Marc Burnouf and his wife, who, with their profound respect for the past, imbue all their handmade pastries with their passion for quality. Before the Maison's present incarnation, complete with a tearoom, it had been producing cakes since the beginning of the last century. The present site, opened in 1990, is charmingly decorated with wooden shelves displaying baskets of almond petit fours, meringues, cookies, shortbread of every variety, homemade breads, and a super-soft brioche made with leaven that is a family recipe dating back to 1907 (and is only available on Sundays), as well as barrels of biscuits as memory-inducing as any of Proust's madeleines. The Burnoufs are not in the least secretive about how all this is produced, and two bay windows on either end of the kitchen afford a view of the family's treats in the making. Tasting is free, and a visit should include a trip to the charming country-style tearoom, where the corner piano is occasionally pressed into service.

Normandy's other temptations include toffees and *balivernes* from Isigny, boiled sweets from Bayeux, Caen, and Falaise, shortbread from Asnelles and Lonlay-l'Abbaye, and chocolates from Calvados. But best of all are the milk-based desserts. The *teurgoules augeronne* is a rice pudding cooked in sweetened milk and flavored with cinnamon, which is left to simmer in the baker's oven. The recipe was devised by sailors' wives at around the time that Honfleur was a major center in the spice trade. It is best eaten with *falues*, a local version of brioche made with crème fraîche, and the Au Bon Pain de Beuvron bakery in the village of Beuvron is an excellent place at which to try it. In 2001, this bakery won first prize for both its *teurgoule* and its *falues*. It is typical of the kind of place one finds in the Pays d'Auge, and Mme Boscher, the owner, also concocts equally delicious cider bread and Normandy apple tarts.

Above: A basket of apples in Calvados. The king of fruit in Normandy, the apple is blessed with many virtues, both gustatory and medicinal. There are no fewer than nine million trees in the Pays d'Auge. The orchard at the Château de Crèvecoeur has twenty-six different varieties of apple trees. Facing page: Main image: Generosity and the warmth of the welcome are the hallmarks at Saint-Vaast-la-Hougue, founded in 1889 in the Cotentin, Gosselin. Top and bottom right: Cider tastings at the Bouche à l'Oreille café and apple and pear local specialties at the grocery in La Perrière.

Originally from the Caucuses and Asia Minor, the apple is one of our oldest fruits. In Normandy, the apple, in all of its myriad varieties, is king, and is credited with every possible virtue. As Patrick Granville says: "It is a fruit that symbolizes life, to bite into an apple is to bite into life itself." Or as another writer, Jean de La Verende, once said: "The apple tree is like the little prince, the heir to the throne of the Normandy countryside. Pear trees flower all at once, but apple trees take their time, and blossom for a full month."

Primary among the uses of the forbidden fruit is the cider that goes so well with so many Norman dishes, including prawns, *andouille de Vire*, cheese, crêpes, and, of course, apple desserts. Cider was introduced during the Middle Ages into the Pays d'Auge in the heart of Calvados, not far from the fashionable seaside resorts (the area is now known as the Route des Pressoirs). Though cider, or *bère* as it is known in Normandy dialect, dates back much further than this and originally came from Biscaye in the Basque region of Spain. Its original name *pomade* derives from the French words for apple (*pomme*) and soul (*âme*), because it was considered a remedy for the afflictions of the spirit. Its composition could not be simpler: one ton of apples for every 200 gallons (750 liters) of water. And it is a genuinely regional and traditional product made on local farms according to strictly ecological principles. The apples are subjected to a series of mechanical pressings to extract their pulp and collected in special baskets known as *resses*. The fruit is then tipped into a granite trough where it is pressed by a horse-drawn wooden grindstone. The *marc*, or *must*, is produced by squeezing this pulp, and the juice from this is then squeezed again. Once fermented, the cider is ready. The best cider, known as the *cidre pur jus* is obtained from the first pressing; subsequent pressings yield the cider consumed on the farm every day. Not unlike champagne—though one must be careful not to upset the producers of the famous sparkling wine, who are particularly sensitive to too many comparisons—there are three types of cider: sweet, dry, and farmhouse, which is an extra-dry variety with a distinctly rustic flavor. Produced in the north of the Manche region, farmhouse cider can reach an alcohol level of 13 percent. Cider is judged under the same criteria as a fine wine, including its color, aroma, and depth, and it is not unusual to hear descriptions such as "nice nose," "fruity," and, "long in the mouth" used in connection with it. Cider is best kept in a cellar at no more than 60°F (15°C), and consumed at a temperature of 45–50°F (8–12°C). Appreciating cider is an art unto itself. Once opened, the liquid remains rather flat in the bottle, but takes on a life all of its own when poured into a glass. More or less sparkling, depending on its provenance, it can be bitter or dry, rough or smooth, with sweet-sour overtones, and the taste of the wood or alcohol more or less evident.

But the use of appless in beverages is by no means confined to cider. There is a range of other beverages derived from the fruit. Pommeau, made from two-thirds apple juice and one-third Calvados, is just one example. Calvados is Normandy's nectar; the essential interlude in one of those interminable but magnificent Sunday lunches that either gives you the energy to continue, or knocks you out, depending on your constitution. This is the famous *Trou Normand*, (the Normandy pause), that in its modern incarnation has become a sorbet doused

Cave
Vins
fins
Spiritueux

Cidre Fermier
de Normandie
CRU DU PAYS DE LA RISLE
René LESUR
Récoltant - Producteur

Above: Bottles of cider from Gribouille in Honfleur. Right: Gribouille's storefront, in a half-timbered house in the town center. Facing page: The Benedictine Museum in Fécamp pays tribute to the liqueur invented in the sixteenth century that uses twenty-seven medicinal plants in its recipe.

with the aforementioned apple brandy. The tradition goes back four hundred years—when a meal is particularly rich, a break accompanied by a glass of calvados has always been de rigueur in Normandy. Aside from its digestive qualities, it quickens the appetite as well as being a wonderful adjunct to a good cheese or a fine cigar as well as making the perfect end to a meal added to a strong black coffee.

In the center of Honfleur, on a street known for its jewelry and home-decoration shops not far from the Eugène Boudin museum, lies Gribouille, known for its always excellent selection of regional produce—although it is their collection of whips suspended from the ceiling that first catches the eye. "It used to be an antiques shop," explains the proprietor. "Nowadays, we have various ciders, vinegars, pear and blackcurrant liqueurs, pommeau, green-apple cream liqueur, and jams. We also have *poiré*, made from pears grown in Domfront and the surrounding woodlands, that is just as good as any of the best ciders and that has become very popular in recent years. It is best drunk very cold, at sunset, when the palate can appreciate the subtle flavors, which can surpass those of the original fruit."

On the coast of the Manche region in the Cotentin, the Gosselin grocery store in Saint-Vast-la-Hougue is run with good humor and a warm sense of hospitality by an owner whose ancestors hail from both Normandy and the Corréze regions. Only just over 400 square feet (40 square meters) in all, the half-timbered structure, situated not far from the town's church, dates back to the eighteenth century. The mullioned window is anything but the classic storefront, though this has not prevented it from attracting a huge following among tourists and locals alike. The original sign above the door translates to "Wood, Lemonade, and Coal," so there was little to suppose that this store would one day be transformed into an elegant establishment offering some of the most delectable foods available. Martine and René Gosselin created this boutique through imagination and hard work, even going so far as to deliver their vegetables and salads on a horse-drawn cart. Nowadays, it is run by their daughter Françoise and her husband, and is a far cry from the large supermarkets that now surround France's cities and towns. Here, the smell of roasting coffee fills the air, foods are lined up alongside natural soaps, packets of biscuits nestle up to tins of sardines, and model boats and still lifes decorate the walls and help create the warm, welcoming atmosphere. The produce all comes from local gardeners, while the biscuits and cakes have an air of New England about them. The soup, on the other hand, is a Gosselin original. Preserves and honeys come in every variety imaginable; the lemon and hazelnut jam, an unusual combination only available here, is concocted by a young local. They are rigorous in their selection process, tasting everything before it is sold, as if to detect the slightest imperfection.

Normandy, home of great workmanship

I n addition to the art of eating well, Normandy sets a standard in the art of good living, with Norman furniture being no exception to this rule. Refined and solid, well crafted, full of character, and easily identifiable. Just as the Austrian, Gustavian, or Provençal styles each possess their own characteristics, Norman furniture has its own set of standards and influences. Indeed, with all its heritage of fine craftsmanship, Normandy has become a region where dealing in secondhand goods has become a general pastime, be it at the antique fairs, flea markets, or the bric-a-brac and tag sales that enliven the summer months throughout the region's villages and seaside resorts.

Béatrice Augié had had enough of life in Paris and her job in communications. So one day she decided to uproot everything, move to Normandy, and become an antiques dealer, opening a shop in one of the hidden gardens in the heart of Deauville. The boutique, appropriately named Le Jardin Secret, occupies the building's ground floor and displays its wares over a concrete floor flooded with daylight pouring through a large glass façade. "It's not the busiest street in town," says Augié, "but perhaps it's better that way." She has also become a decorator with her own interior design practice, and now devotes a space in her shop to fabrics. There is nothing fussy here, only solid, simple furniture in stripped oak that she picks up in Belgium, and also kilim-upholstered foot stools, sofas from Caravanes, and a selection of lamps.

In her shop in Boissy-Maugis, located in the Le Perche region, Anne-Marie Mesnil knows the art of transmitting her passion for beautiful things. In her white-walled shop with pastel woodwork and decorative mirrors that she made herself, she cleverly combines the old with the new. Porcelain, bamboo chairs, cane armchairs, ceramics by Jean-Baptiste Astier de Villatte, and rainbow-colored lemonade glasses, along with paintings and pieces by friends and artists whose work she promotes—for example, Jean Boggio, and his enamels designed for Longwy—are shown here. The shop spills out into a garden, cleverly designed by the landscape artist Marc Julien. Wisteria casts its spell in the courtyard, while in the pond a cascade of water dances on the stone. This antiques shop (formerly a butcher shop) has become a haven of tranquility, with the added attractions of a bookshop and tearoom.

Seduced by the charms of La Perrière, three friends, all fed up with the stress of big-city life, created a special space selling engraved glasses alongside bracelets from Rajasthan. The adjoining tearoom also abounds in unusual associations and offers jam and homemade cakes. The designer Chantal Thomass, who owns a house in the village, helped a little with the shop's decor. "A modest contribution as proof of my fondness for the place," she confides.

Left: An antiques shop, famous for its collection of bonsai trees, in Condeau near to Rémalard in Perche.
Facing page clockwise from top left: Béatrice Augié's boutique Le Jardin Secret in Deauville. Anne-Marie Mesnil's in Boisy-Maugis. The Fassier house in Rémalard is located in a former parochial school. Ethnic objects, industrial furniture, and curiosities at the Moulin de la Pleugère. Fireside and garden implements in enamel are sold in the antiques corner of the Manoir de Lormarin. Garden furniture in the Fassier house.

In Normandy, terra-cotta has a lengthy history of being functional; but, above all, it has been used decoratively, even allegorically. In its functional role, there are pots, jugs, clothes irons, plates, and foot-warmers. In its allegorical guise, one finds it used to decorate façades, to cobble walls, and in religious emblems, such as windows, finials, and cemetery crosses. First introduced in 1664, earthenware production was concentrated in Rouen, but also in Mélamare in the Seine-Maritime, Infreville in the Eure, and in Martincamp. For some time, the blue design on a white background, inspired by Delft porcelain and Chinese kaolin, was the order of the day, until red became incorporated at the end of the seventeenth century. Old Rouen was born. In the capital of Haute-Normandie, tastes wavered between terra-cotta treasures and the marvels of medicine: in the Ceramics Museum, the terra-cotta pharmacy jars rival the celestial spheres of the Pierre Chapelle. The production of enameled terra-cotta in Pré-d'Auge would later add a fourth hue to the famous three already in use—a green or yellow glaze, with a lovely glow produced naturally by the effect of light. From that time on, the art of ceramics became richer, more complex and diversified into *rocaille*, a whimsical decorative style that became fashionable in the eighteenth century. The evolution of their designs was another factor; motifs were enriched with arabesques and details borrowed from embroidery and ironwork. At this time, Rouen was at its peak, but England saw to it that this changed—the eternal rivalry once more coming into play. This time, the English won the day and took over the porcelain market, putting an end to Norman production. What is more, it was an Englishman, George Wood, who introduced ceramics to Forges-les-Eaux, one of the leading centers of Norman glazed earthenware.

But the Bray region was not left behind as a producer. Indeed, the etymology of the name Bray is not irrelevant to the creative destiny of the area, since the term means mud in Celtic. One town in the region remains a pioneer—Forges-les-Eaux, with its production of heavy earthenware known as Vieux Forges, and a range of white, gracefully decorated crockery, also produced in shades of sky blue or amethyst.

Porcelain from Bayeux, Valognes, and Isigny is today considered museum quality. Apart from its production of garden gnomes, which is best forgotten, Noron-la-Poterie excels in the art of terra-cotta, as its name suggests. The town's output is known for its distinctive color, derived from the salt sandstone that confers the famous brown hue on every piece. The majority of Norman household crockery is made here: the Saint-Gorgon cider pitcher; the *bobin* milk pot; the *guichon* individual soup tureen; the *mahon*, in which eggs and foods were once kept cool; and the small calvados jug, a little kitsch perhaps, but full of local color, with its matching tasting cups and cork in the shape of a woman's head. Valognes also is known for its terra-cotta pottery. The *gohan* is a famous piece—a soup tureen that originated in England, where the peasants would use it to bring soup to the fields.

And finally, moving on to more lofty creations—though these too are made from clay—one mustn't forget the finials used to decorate the dormer windows that punctuate the roofs of many Norman houses.

Above: One of the creations from the pottery at Mesnil de Bavent is this enameled roof tile. Facing page: Main image: The pottery studio and some of the handmade items produced here. Top: Medallions and fleurs de lis decorate the façade. Center and bottom: The finials are inspired by Renaissance-era designs and are used to decorate rooftops throughout Normandy.

Normandy's little museums

Above: The well opposite Jean-François Millet's family home in Gréville-Hague on the Manche coast. Facing page: Main image: The painter's bedroom remains unchanged. An ascetic ambience akin to a monk's cell reigns here, with its wooden bed and country furniture that doubtless contributed to the spare style of his paintings. Top: Earthenware pots and dishes engraved with the famous painting "The Angelus". Center and bottom: A collection of stoneware and glass jugs.

Suspended in time, these museums—far from the sometimes overwhelming splendor of the big national museums—give the visitor the impression that they are gently rolling back the years. Lost in the countryside or hidden behind the half-timbered façade of a town house, they beguile us with their unusual and picturesque charm. The two large towns of Caen and Rouen have large museums with prestigious collections set in former manor houses. But there are the smaller museums, which, like a photo album or a scrapbook, provide a window onto the many facets of Norman life through the ages, as seen through its arts and crafts. Take for example Gréville-Hague, Jean-François Millet's house. Here, both the furniture and the interior decoration are traditional. It is a small stone house, simple and rustic, imbued with the same solitude that is found in the artist's paintings.

The Norman style is both provincial and sophisticated, ingenuous and refined, reflecting some of the contradictions of the region itself. Evocations of these seemingly paradoxical qualities abound in its houses and castles, with their creaking wooden floors and multitude of traditional armoires. The seventeenth century saw the apotheosis of cabinetmaking in Normandy. Production was concentrated around Caen, Fécamp, and Yvetot. Here too, that precise period played a determining role in the style of furniture. Modest and unostentatious when times were hard, it took on a more flamboyant style when the economy started to flourish. In the seventeenth and the nineteenth centuries, decoration was at its height, and metaphors of love and abundance were the order of the day. Sheaves of wheat, horns of plenty, grapes, hearts, acanthus leaves, and musical instruments were all employed. Arrows and doves symbolized love, torches symbolized marriage, and birds' nests the family, while the pelican denoted piety. The various woods used included naturally treated oak, pine, elm, apple wood, chestnut, and beech.

The first criterion used to judge the quality of a piece of Norman furniture was the preciousness of the wood employed. Its solidity was considered a sign of timelessness and tradition. Next, was how the wood was worked: it could be left plain, without any ornamentation, with time being it's only embellishment—the luster of age on a beautiful piece of oak for example or it could be a carefully carved piece, worked into something delicate and refined. The Louis XIII sideboard with carved doors, cutlery drawers, and turned legs is one example; the cupboard, first introduced at the beginning of the seventeenth century, is another. Often placed on a sideboard, its design was perfectly functional. In elm, pine, cherry, or, more often than not, oak, its shelves can be smooth or carefully carved, with cornices and balustrades to hold the crockery and display the most decorative plates.

Tables in Normandy abound in rustic charm, so much so that they are often given the sobriquet "harvest tables," while traditional chairs have a particular style that began to emerge from the eighteenth century onward.

Another pinnacle in Norman furniture design is the grandfather clock, which comes in every conceivable shape and form. There is the basket clock, decorated with baskets of fruit and flowers; the pendulum clock; coffin-shaped clocks; and clocks with flat backs or in the shape of an inverted pyramid. The Saint-Nicolas clock, with its lavishly decorated orb, is named after the town of that name, while the ladies clock, slender and with a glass front, is peculiar to Caen. These types of clocks are also referred to as parquet clocks, because they tended to be placed in the main living room. The body of the clock was usually in pine, cherry, or oak, and the dial in bronze, pewter, copper, or even white enamel. The only "foreign" parts are the interior mechanisms, which sometimes come from the Jura region of France or from Switzerland.

Finally, there is the Normandy wardrobe—the grandfather of Normandy furniture and the progenitor of all that followed—that first made its appearance in the thirteenth century. Made of solid oak, it is often crowned with a carved cornice depicting flowers, fruit, doves, and sheaves of wheat, and can have up to two drawers in its base. It is the classic wedding gift, the perfect chest for the bride's trousseau, especially if it is embellished with a Cupid's quiver, a dove's nest, or a bouquet of roses symbolizing happiness.

The Château de Martainville, located outside Rouen in the Seine-Maritime, houses a fine selection of rare pieces of antique furniture. Built in the sixteenth century, the estate stretches from the Robec valley to the edge of the forest at Lyons. In 1485, Jacques Le Pelletier built his residence here, and it was finally purchased by the state in 1906 and converted it into a museum some sixty years later. In 1571, the Martainville family bought the property, and it was passed down through the female line of the family throughout the eighteenth century. The grounds are a fine example of life at that time; in addition to a dovecote, there is also a carriage house and a bread oven. While a visit here is warranted for the Renaissance atmosphere of the château alone, the real interest lies in the museum dedicated to traditional arts and crafts in Normandy, and its comprehensive collection of traditional Norman furniture dating from the Middle Ages through the Second Empire. The museum is an homage to the extraordinary cultural diversity of the region: four floors of exhibition space have retained their original layout and magnificent fireplaces, as well as housing some of the finest objects made from the fifteenth to the nineteenth centuries. On the first floor, pewter, copper, pottery, ceramics, glassware, stoneware, and popular earthenware from Forges-les-Eaux are exhibited alongside re-creations of the interiors of country cottages from Bray, the Caux, and the Eure regions, as well as examples from the coast. Renaissance trunks are displayed next to nineteenth-century

Above: Collections from the Château de Pont-Rilly and the Normandy Folklore Museum on display at the Château de Martainville, near Rouen. Pewter, copper, and earthenware from Forges-les-Eaux.
Facing page: Main image: The museum is housed in a Renaissance-inspired château. Top: The carved wooden face of a traditional Normandy clock. A wardrobe's doors embellished with carved baskets of flowers as an augury of wealth. Center: Often in oak, they are also to be found in elm and sometimes even in apple wood. Bottom: Another item specific to Normandy and its craftsmen is this raised four-poster bed with sliding doors.

Above, top: The Victor Hugo Museum at Villequier. This red-brick house overlooking the Seine was built in 1820. It had a shed, stables, and half-timbered outbuildings. Originally, the garden stretched as far as the river. There is an air of tragedy to this house, since it was here that Hugo wrote his "Contemplations" inspired by the death of his daughter, Léopoldine, and her husband, Charles Vacquerie, who drowned in 1843. Below, left and right: A visit to the museum dedicated to La Dame aux Camélias in Gacé is an immersion into the Romantic era. Facing page: At the museum devoted to traditional mercantile and trade businesses in Lignerolles, the displays, from privately held collections, pay tribute to the shops and professions of a bygone era. Following page: The Manoir des Milles Feuilles in the Pays d'Auge.

carved wooden wardrobes, clocks from Beaubec-la-Rosière, and trundle beds from the seventeenth and nineteenth centuries. The third floor is devoted to a detailed analysis of traditional eighteenth-century Norman costumes, complete with their accompanying bonnets, jewelry, and lace.

A small museum in Lignerolles in the Orne is devoted to traditional mercantile and trading businesses and is a more down-to-earth sort of place. A dozen rooms have been transformed into traditional shops including a haberdashery, a grocery, a hairdresser, and a pub. One can view kitchen utensils, old advertisements, and decorative items dating from the first half of the twentieth century, as well. Some twenty thousand items in all, many donated from private collections, make up a fascinating collection that is tastefully and carefully orchestrated with a deep sense of respect for the heritage it portrays.

Built between 1626 and 1636, the Château Balleroy in Calvados was built with the local materials—gray stone and red schist. It was one of François Mansart's first commissions. Mansart also designed the church on the grounds of the château. Acquired by the Forbes family, it now houses the Hot Air Balloon museum, and is the focal point for an event known as "Those Magnificent Men in Their Flying Machines," where amateur aviators take to the air in contraptions of their own design. The garden, designed by Le Nôtre, is as strictly symmetrical as one would expect, and the interior no less rigorously planned and executed. Nineteenth-century hunting scenes, painted by Count Albert de Balleroy, line the walls of the ground floor living rooms, and the wooden paneling in the dining room illustrates fables from La Fontaine. The silk hangings in one of the upstairs bedrooms are identical to those found in the Grand Trianon in Versailles.

In Gacé, not far from Nonant-le-Pin where she was born, and close to the Argentelles Manor on the border of the Ouche and the Pays d'Auge, is a most interesting museum devoted to the Lady of the Camelias. Relics and mementos of the most famous and most romantic courtesan of all time are housed here. The first room has been transformed into a theater where a silhouette of Lizt plays the piano while a slide show displays the various places that marked her life from her birth in the Orne to her death in Paris at the age of 23 from tuberculosis—the wasting disease said to afflict those who die for love. Also featured is the Château de la Roche in Cochère, where, under the name Marie Duplesis, she lived with the Duke of Narbonne; as well as the church of Saint-Germain at Clairefeuille where she made her first communion. The second room displays jewelry, tableware, and costumes from the Paris Opéra that were used in Verdi's retelling of her story, *La Traviata*. There are also various personal papers, passports, and amulets that may seem like mere trinkets, but are quite enough to evoke the intrigue and romanticism of a life lived for the moment, without thought for tomorrow. The last room is devoted to memorabilia—posters, photographs, and films—of the many artists who have portrayed this tragic figure, including Sarah Bernhardt, Greta Garbo, Maria Callas, and Isabelle Adjani.

Those who love the sea, white cliffs, narrow paths hidden in the depths of the countryside, lush forests, elegant towns, or tiny fishing villages, will not be disappointed by Normandy and its many riches. With the help of this guide, you can discover bed-and-breakfasts in cottages with flourishing gardens, traditional timber-framed residences, or sophisticated hotels with a view of the sea. Stop by little bistros, tearooms, and bakeries to sample delicious Norman specialties that feature butter and cream, as well as ocean-fresh oysters and fish best enjoyed with local ciders and *pommeau*, the local apple liqueur. Stock up on cheeses and other famous regional products in small specialty stores. Browse through the wares of antique shops, order stained glass or finials for your country home, or stroll through the many gardens and small museums. This is the place for a memorable holiday, long or short, between the sea and the countryside.

Below, you will find the addresses for all the places mentioned throughout this book that are open to the public, as well as many others recommended by the authors.

No addresses are given for Le Havre or Cherbourg, as visitors wishing to discover the essence of the region will presumably prefer to keep to the smaller towns and villages.

A vast region, Normandy spans five départements, from Mont-Saint-Michel, in the southwest extremity of the region, to Le Touquet, in the northeast. The addresses in this guide are set out according to département, with each section arranged in alphabetical order according to the towns and villages.

Naturally, it would be impossible to provide an exhaustive list of addresses, given the region's countless tiny guesthouses off small roads and innumerable bed-and-breakfasts in apple tree-dotted farms, or stately homes and castles. This necessarily selective listing is limited to the places that particularly enchanted the authors of this book.

The hotels located by the sea or in the heart of the countryside are often magnificent eighteenth-century residences, town houses, or beautifully restored farmhouses that exude a sense of timelessness. With the exception of large hotels, catering facilities are not always available, but this is not a problem as visitors have a range of fine restaurants nearby to choose from. Elegantly formal or charmingly homey, good Norman eateries offer all types of local products prepared in the traditional way.

Many of the bed-and-breakfasts are family-run affairs, each with its own history. Whether you prefer to be cradled in the serenity of the countryside or invigorated by sea breezes, bed-and-breakfasts allow you to enjoy a unique holiday experience close to nature, with the opportunity to spend solitary moments far from the fashionable resorts.

As in all books in this series, large art museums do not appear in this section, as they are already featured in most tourist guides and brochures.

SEINE-MARITIME

HOTELS

CHÂTEAU DE SASSETOT
Route départementale 5
76540 Sassetot le Mauconduit
Tel.: + 33 (0)2 35 28 00 11
(see photo page 157)
Situated in a park not far from the beach of Petites Dalles, this spacious and beautiful classic residence was made famous by one of its prestigious clients, Sissi, Empress of Austria.

CHÂTEAU DE VILLEQUIER
76490 Villequier
Tel: + 33 (0)2 35 95 94 10
www.chateau-de-villequier.com
The view of the Seine and the countryside from the Château is impressive, as is its entranceway through the forest. Adding to the charm is the dovecote between the residence and the somewhat austere rooms in ivy-covered outbuildings. The extremely hospitable lady of the manor further contributes to the fantastic atmosphere of the place.

DORMY HOUSE
Route du Havre, 76790 Étretat
Tel: + 33 (0)2 35 27 07 88,
Fax: + 33 (0)2 35 29 86 19
Email: dormy.house@wanadoo.fr
www.dormy-house.com
Perched on a rock, this residence overlooks the sea and the town of Étretat. A three-star hotel in a magnificent building where terraces are gently caressed by the sun as sea breezes sweep across the bay.

DOUCE FRANCE
13, rue du Docteur Girard
76980 Veules les Roses,
Tel: + 33 (0)2 35 57 85 30
Email: contact@doucefrance.fr
In this village filled with timber-framed houses, this beautiful eighteenth-century coaching house is now a charming hotel with a very British feel. The bedrooms or little suites (with a living room, bedroom and kitchen) overlook the flowery courtyard or the Veule, the smallest river in France.

LA FERME DE LA CHAPELLE
Côte de la Vierge, 76400 Fécamp
Tel: + 33 (0)3 35 10 12 12
The Eglise Notre Dame du Salut dominates the town of Fécamp from the top of a cliff.

Attached to this chapel that offers a spectacular view of all the cliffs up to the Cap d'Autifer, is an old farm that has been transformed into a hotel. The rooms are simple, with some opening directly onto a garden with a beautiful swimming pool in the courtyard framed by stone and flint farm buildings. A pleasant and secluded spot, ideal for those with children.

HOTEL LE GRAND PAVOIS
15, quai Vicomté, 76400 Fécamp
Tel: + 33 (0)2 35 10 01 01
Email: legrandpavois@wanadoo.fr
For lovers of modern architecture and design, here are some rooms with a very contemporary flavor that offer a view of the boats in the port, just near the walkway along the beach.

HOTEL DE LA PLAGE
92, rue Jean Heuze, 76540 Les Petites Dalles
Tel: + 33 (0)2 35 27 40 77
In the heart of a village with attractive brick and flint houses, this hotel is located at the bottom of the cliff, not far from a little beach with a pretty line of cabins. Note that the hotel restaurant is excellent, with a chef who has a way with regional products.

HOTEL DES ROCHERS
Place de la Libération,
76740 Sotteville-sur-mer
Tel: + 33 (0)2 35 97 07 06
In the middle of a wall-enclosed garden, this tiny hotel is located in a former presbytery next to the church in an extremely peaceful village. The path to the sea has a steep staircase that leads down to a lovely pebble beach.

BED-AND-BREAKFASTS

ABBAYE SAINT-WANDRILLE DE FONTENELLE
76490 Saint-Wandrille-Rançon
Tel: + 33 (0)2 35 96 23 11
Email: st-wandrille@wanadoo.fr
From the original edifice, only the north transept remains. The cloister's Renaissance interior and the New Testament scenes decorating the refectory door have also survived the passage of time. Benedictine monks have lived here since 1931. The abbey offers lodging to those wishing to taste the serenity of monastic life.

CHÂTEAU DES AYGNES
Route de Fécamp, 76790 Étretat
Tel: + 33 (0)2 35 28 92 77

On the road to Fécamp you will find this holiday residence built in the 1860s—a rare example of resort architecture from the earliest era of seaside vacations. Nineteenth-century novelist Guy de Maupassant describes it in his text on Étretat. Open for visits, the château offers two tastefully furnished guest rooms. For a very pleasant stay in a beautiful spot with a sea view, surrounded by a recently restored garden.

CHÂTEAU DU MESNIL GEOFFROY
76740 Ermenouville
Tel: + 33 (0)2 35 57 12 77
Email: contact@chateau-mesnil-geoffroy.com
Princess Anne-Marie Kayali
The château has kept intact its seventeenth-century décor with period furniture and family heirlooms. Wooden objects, floor tiles with corner squares, Versailles wood flooring—these are the elements that set the tone of the large living rooms and five lavishly decorated bedrooms. Meals served here are as delectable as the gorgeous setting. Visiting the rose garden is another high point of this venue.

FERME DE BRAY
76440 Sommery
Tel: + 33 (0)2 35 90 57 27
Email: ferme.de.bray@wanadoo.fr
Liliane and Patrice Perrier
Near Forges-les-Eaux, you will come across this stone dwelling with a magnificently restored façade that dates back to the seventeenth century. The property contains a waterwheel, a bread-oven, a dovecote and a cider press. All this in the heart of lush, hilly countryside. With five bedrooms available and exhibitions regularly organized on the ground floor.

FERME DE L'ECOSSE
76 110 Manneville la Goupil
Tel: + 33 (0)2 35 27 77 21
Monsieur and Madame Loisel
An eighteenth-century construction located eight miles (13 km) from Étretat, with lovely spacious rooms overlooking the garden. A place overflowing with souvenirs cherished by the owner Nicole Loisel.

LA HOSANNIERE
Chemin du Simplon,
76740 La Chapelle-sur-Dun
Tel: + 33 (0)2 35 97 44 59
Email: lahosanniere@fnac.net
Martine Dophat-Latour

English Channel

Côte d'Albâtre

Côte d'Albâtre

Varengeville-sur-Mer
Dieppe

Saint-Valery-
en-Caux
Sainte-Marguerite-
sur-Mer

Pays de Bray

Auderville
La Hague
Beaumont-Hague
Vauville
Cherbourg
Barfleur
Quettehou
Saint-Vaast-la-Hougue
Island Tatihou

Cany-Barville
Durdent

Fécamp

Pays de Caux

Étretat

Bellevue

SEINE-MARITIME

Bricquebec
Valognes
Sainte-Mère-Église

Cotentin

Côte de Nacre

Le Havre

Villequier

Jumièges
Rouen

UPPER NORMANDY

Carteret

Portbail

Douve

Isigny-sur-Mer

Courseulles-sur-Mer
Côte Fleurie
Côte de Grâce
Honfleur
Deauville
Trouville-sur-Mer

Pont-Audemer
La Bouille

Norman Vexin

Elbeuf

Arromanches-les-Bains

Cabourg
Houlgate
Pont-l'Évêque

Risle

Ouistreham

Bayeux

Dives-sur-Mer
Beaumont-en-Auge

Le Bec-Hellouin

Louviers

Seine

Giverny

MANCHE

Caen

Beuvron-en-Auge
Pays d'Auge

Lisieux

Bernay

EURE

Eure

Saint-Lô

Coutances

Vire

CALVADOS

Swiss Normandy

Livarot
Orbec

Touques

Beaumont-le-Roger

Évreux

Regnéville-sur-Mer

Sienne

LOWER NORMANDY

Pays d'Ouche

Granville

Vire

Falaise

Dives

Gacé

Villedieu-les-Poêles

Orne

Argentan

Mont-Saint-Michel
Avranches

ORNE

Couesnon
Sélune

Bagnoles-de-l'Orne

Mortagne-au-Perche

Alençon

Perche

0   20 km
© map: **Edigraphie**

MANOIR DE VILLERS

30 Route de Sahurs
76113 Saint-Pierre-de-Manneville
Tel: + 33 (0)2 35 32 07 02
www.manoirdevillers.com
The Manoir de Villers was, in 1581, a feudal domain with several dependencies. Enlarged from the sixteenth to nineteenth centuries, it became the largest existing manor in France. The truly unique park, created in the eighteenth century before being extended and reworked in the nineteenth century, has been restored. With a real passion for their home, the friendly owners personally show visitors around on guided tours of the manor.

VILLA LES CHARMETTES

Allée des Pervenches, 76790 Étretat
Tel: + 33 (0)2 35 27 05 54
Cellphone: + 33 (0)6 88 15 29 76
Madame Renard
A pretty villa on the heights of the town, elegantly decorated by its young, dynamic owners who welcome travelers to their family home for a minimum of two nights.

LE VIEUX CARRE

Allée des Pervenches, 76790 Étretat
Tel: + 33 (0)2 35 27 05 54
Cellphone: + 33 (0)6 88 15 29 76
A small timber-framed house in the heart of historic Rouen. Tastefully decorated, certain rooms overlook the charming courtyard that doubles as a tearoom when the weather permits.

RESTAURANTS AND BISTROS

RESTAURANT GILL
8 and 9, quai de la Bourse
76000 Rouen
Tel: + 33 (0)2 35 71 16 14
A gastronomic delight in a contemporary
setting, offering delicious modern dishes.
Mentioned in the *Relais Gourmands* guide.

RESTAURANT LA SALAMANDRE
4, Boulevard René Coty, 76790 Étretat
Tel: + 33 (0)2 35 27 17 07
The only macrobiotic brasserie in all of
Normandy is found in a medieval house in the
heart of Étretat. Here, farm products are used,
and seafood is fished from ecological waters.
Once situated in Lisieux, the residence was
taken apart, then reconstructed in Étretat.
It also houses a hotel, La Résidence.

UN JOUR D'ETE
25, rue Victor Hugo, 76980 Veules-les-Roses
Tel: + 33 (0)2 35 97 23 17
A delightful tearoom with a sunny little courtyard,
in a quaint village. Here, meals are light, the
sandwiches scrumptious, the cakes refined, the
newspapers and regional guidebooks numerous.
A very cozy place. (see photo page 178)

LES VIEUX PLATS
76280 Gonneville-la-Mallet
Tel: + 33 (0)2 35 20 72 27
Time has come to a standstill in this big house
with pebble-dashed walls found in the town
center. Here, the décor is astonishing: wooden
objects painted with frescoes, portraits,
landscapes, flowers, and a large full-figure
portrait of the owner's grandfather. Bookings
are required for lunch, served on Sunday only,
but it is possible to have a coffee here every
day of the week. The owner also opens the
door of his kitchen to clients: the impressive
stove is 150 years old! (see photo page 176)

GOURMET STORES

LE RENDEZ-VOUS
DES GOURMANDS
47, rue de la Barre, 76200 Dieppe
Tel: + 33 (0)2 35 40 11 94
Laureen and Cesidio di Andréa left Paris
and their restaurant in the capital's ninth
arrondissement for this charming Godin-equipped
kitchen. From its eight stoves and two ovens flow
mountains of *madeleines* and poppy-jam muffins.
The shop offers a selection of Italian products,

cornflower syrup, perfumed spices, and soon, the
divine flavors of the Palais des Thés tea range.

OLIVIER
18, rue Saint-Jacques, 76200 Dieppe
Tel: + 33 (0)2 35 84 22 55
One of the last stores of its kind in France—
a grocery store, cheese shop, wine cellar
and roast coffee-bean seller. The boutique is
found just near the pedestrian road, between
the Eglise Saint-Jacques and the Café des
Tribunaux. A passionate defender of his unique
and authentic store, Monsieur Olivier pays
meticulous attention to all his wares.

PATISSERIE A LA DUCHESSE
DE BERRY
212 Grande Rue, 76200 Dieppe
Tel: + 33 (0)2 35 84 21 93
Delicious cakes and pastries from the region and
elsewhere are on offer in this elegant patisserie
where tea is also served in the afternoon.

PATISSERIE GERARD LECŒUR
47, rue Alphonse Karr, 76790 Étretat
Tel: + 33 (0)2 35 27 02 54
The region's star patisserie also features a tearoom
where you can taste delicacies such as the
addictive almond and hazelnut *normandines* or
the luscious *marguerites* with orange-flower water.
All this in a refined, airy space that exudes old-
fashioned elegance. (see photo page 183)

SMALL MUSEUMS

ABBAYE DE JUMIEGES
24, rue Guilaume le Conquérant
76480 Jumièges,
Tel: + 33 (0)2 35 37 24 02
A magnificent example of Romanesque art with
a ninety-foot-high (27 m) nave open to the sky.
The remains of the capitulary room, the two
octagonal towers, the twelfth-century wine
cellar, and the abbatial lodgings have survived,
though they have suffered significant ruin over
the centuries. The abbey is found in the middle
of an orchard.

ABBAYE SAINT-GEORGES
DE BOSCHERVILLE
76840 Saint-Martin-de-Boscherville
Tel: + 33 (0)2 35 32 10 82
The abbey was built in 1125, yet its lovely
façade composed of immaculate stones still
gleams brightly. A large tower and two turrets
grace the edifice. The motifs on the prominent
gate, the windows of the nave, and the fine

lines of the caps of the columns contribute to
the mystique of the place.

MAISON MAURICE LEBLANC
Clos Arsène Lupin, 15, rue Guy de Maupassant
76790 Étretat
Tel: + 33 (0)2 35 10 59 53
In 1919, novelist Maurice Leblanc—creator
of Arsène Lupin, the fictional gentleman-thief—
bought Le Sphinx, a house he would rename Le
Clos Lupin. Built in 1850, the house is a model
of great Norman architecture, featuring crossed
timber frames, wooden cornices, a balcony,
bow windows framed by caryatids, and a lush
garden where sweet-smelling roses grow.

MANOIR D'ANDRE GIDE
Cuverville-en-Caux, 76280 Criquetot-l'Esneval
Tel: + 33 (0)2 35 29 15 08
The façade of the residence is graced by
twenty or so windows. Visible brickwork,
white stones and a slate roof also characterize
this austere house, rich in souvenirs, that the
eminent writer mentions in *If It Die*, written in
1926. Fellow writers Paul Valéry, Charles Bos,
and André Maurois also frequented this house,
meeting place of the group that, in 1909, gave
birth to the French literary journal *La Nouvelle
Revue Française*.

MUSEE DE LA CERAMIQUE
Rue Faucon, 76000 Rouen
Tel: + 33 (0)2 35 07 31 74
Here, the whimsical quality of the pharmacy
pots rivals with the lyricism of the heavenly
spheres in stone.

MUSEE PIERRE CORNEILLE
502 rue Pierre Corneille, 76650 Petit-Couronne
Tel: + 33 (0)2.35.68.13.89
On the first floor, the study of the seventeenth-
century dramatist has been recreated, with
a walnut-wood armchair (a copy of the
seventeenth-century original) decorated with
a wool and silk tapestry illustrating one of the
scenes from *The Golden Fleece*. As if encasing
a relic in a shrine, a glass window protects
a 1658 edition of Corneille's translation of
the *Imitation of Christ* by Thomas à Kempis.
In the bedroom is the canopy bed with velvet
hangings where Corneille apparently snuggled
under an enormous pile of blankets. Also on
display is a sauna—a perfect place to reflect. In
the garden are a thatch-roofed bake-house and
the vegetable garden created in the seventeenth
century. Behind the house mingle the shadows
of apple trees, pear trees and hazelnut trees.

MUSEE DES TRADITIONS
ET ARTS NORMANDS
Château de Martainville
76116 Martainville-Epreuville
Tel: + 33 (0)2 35 23 44 70
The museum presents a moving retrospective of
Norman life. On the ground floor and the first
floor, you will find wardrobes, cupboards,
clocks from the fifteenth to the nineteenth
centuries; on the second floor, rustic furniture,
Martincamp pottery, glassware from the Vallée
de la Bresle and ceramics from Forges-les-Eaux;
and finally, on the third floor, local costumes.
(see photos pages 196–197)

MUSEE VICTOR HUGO
Rue Ernest Binet, 76490 Villequier
Tel: + 33 (0)2 35 56 91 86
Victor Hugo and his family lived in this
dwelling on the banks of the Seine, where
fascinating traces of his life, poetic souvenirs,
drawings and writings, are now displayed.

PALAIS BENEDICTINE-FECAMP
110, rue Alexandre Le Grand, 76400 Fécamp
Tel: + 33 (0)2 35 10 26 10
Created in 1863 by an alcohol merchant called
Alexandre Le Grand, this palace adjoining the
Benedictine factory houses a museum where
you can browse through posters singing the
praises of the plant-based liqueur invented by
monks of the former Abbaye de Fécamp. A real
architectural marvel, this factory-palace was
conceived by Camille Albert, who, inspired by
fellow architect Viollet-le-Duc, juxtaposed Neo-
Gothic and Renaissance styles. An abundance
of collections awaits visitors: ivory, Nottingham
alabaster, statues, manuscripts, fifteenth-century
prayer books, illuminations, oil lamps, and a
sumptuous *Sleeping Virgin*, a bas-relief in
polychrome wood dating from the end of the
fifteenth century. (see photo page 188)

PAVILLON GUSTAVE FLAUBERT
(DE CROISSET)
18, quai Gustave-Flaubert, Dieppedale-Croisset
76380 Canteleu
Tel: + 33 (0)2 35 36 43 91
Though the original residence of the famous
nineteenth-century novelist has disappeared,
the garden pavilion still stands. Called the
"petit salon" (little salon), this is where
discussions were held; when conversation
waned, guests only had to lift their heads to
admire the stars. On evenings with a full moon,
the writer recited his verses on the terrace
skirted by lime-blossom trees. During the day,

he went canoeing and jotted down ideas for his works. Inside the house, the only remaining personal effects are some goose-feather quills, clay pipes, a paper cutter, a pot of tobacco, an inkpot in the shape of a toad, several locks of hair, and the handkerchief with which Flaubert apparently wiped his brow before dying. His library was claimed by the municipal council of Canteleu-Croisset.

PARKS AND GARDENS

AGAPANTHE
76850 Grigneuseville
Tel: + 33 (0)2 35 33 32 05
Right next to Tôtes, between Rouen and Dieppe, you will find this beautiful garden with an eclectic mix of flowers, hellebores, hydrangeas, and romantic waterside spots.

LE BOIS DES MOUTIERS
76119 Varengeville-sur-Mer
Tel: + 33 (0)2 35 85 10 02
One of the most famous parks in Normandy, featuring camellias, azaleas, hydrangeas and rhododendrons orchestrated by English landscape artist Gertrude Jekyll. The house designed by architect Edwin Lutyens at the start of the twentieth century in the Arts and Crafts style, is situated at the heart of this exceptional domain. (see photos pages 112–115)

CHÂTEAU DE BOSMELET
76720 Auffay
Tel: + 33 (0)2 35 32 81 07
The vegetable garden is called the "arc-en-ciel" (rainbow) and each plot of land has been named after a precious stone—"ambre" (amber), "saphir" (sapphire), "grenat" (garnet), "ivoire" (ivory). The domain was badly in need of a bit of brightening up as it almost did not survive the war bombings. After taking over from her mother-in-law, the current lady of the manor Laurence de Bosmelet breathed new life into the place by drawing inspiration from the original seventeenth-century plans. The vegetable garden now includes two hundred zucchini, five hundred cabbages, one thousand seven hundred broccolis and cauliflowers. Her sinologist husband has also created his own Asian-inspired vegetable garden that grows in a peaceful atmosphere.

CHÂTEAU DE MIROMESNIL
76550 Tourville-sur-Arques
Tel: + 33 (0)2 35 85 02 80
An English-style garden with vegetables, fruit

trees, flowers and clematis plants. A sixteenth-century chapel can be found on the far end of the beech tree forest. (see photos pages 72–73)

CLOS DU COUDRAY
14, rue du Parc floral, 76850 Etaimpuis
Tel: + 33 (0)2 35 34 96 85
A garden made up of floral marvels from the ends of the earth, following the length of a river. A botanical and visual delight, organized according to color and species.

JARDINS D'ANGELIQUE
Manoir de Montmains, Route de Lyons
76520 Montmain
Tel: + 33 (0)2 35 79 08 12
An angelic serenity reigns over this garden not far from Rouen, which is visited for its ancient roses and pastel flowers. A seventeenth-century manor house and a sheepfold provide a pretty backdrop.

JARDINS DE BELLEVUE
76850 Beaumont-le-Hareng
Tel: + 33 (0)2 35 33 31 37
Between Rouen and Dieppe stands this English-style landscaped garden—fifty acres (20 ha) filled with hellebores, hydrangeas, clematis plants, lilies, and primroses. A place for beautiful strolls not far from Tôtes.

JARDIN LA COQUETTERIE
Frontebosc, 76570 Limesy
Tel: + 33 (0)2 35 91 28 01
Thirty-six squares (two yards by two yards), each occupied by a single flower, herb or vegetable, with the configuration changing regularly, as is the rule in any self-respecting vegetable garden. A waltz of thyme, garlic, chives, basil, oregano, parsley, sage, cornflowers, pansies, and asters. And as tenderness often holds everything together, Pascal Cribier has filled in spaces with terra-cotta pots containing love apples. Bushes pruned into spheres and a bench by sculptor Claude Lalanne add further artistic touches to the place.

JARDIN DES PLANTES
114 ter, avenue des Martyrs de la Résistance
76000 Rouen
Tel: + 33 (0)2 35 72 36 36
The property stretches out over twenty-five acres (10 ha) and includes an eighteenth-century pavilion, an orange grove, and above all, a tropical greenhouse built in the nineteenth century that houses plants bearing an eerie likeness to alien life forms.

JARDIN PLUME
76116 Auzouville sur Ry
Tel/fax: + 33 (0)2 35 23 00 01
The most famous lawn garden in all of Normandy. (see photo page 91)

JARDIN SHAMROCK
Route du manoir d'Ango
76119 Varengeville-sur-Mer
Tel: + 33 (0)2 35 85 14 64
One of the most beautiful hydrangea collections in the Pays de Caux, created in 1983. Corinne Mallet picks up her plants from all over the world, in particular from Japan. Her garden was born in 1990 and baptized Shamrock in memory of a trip to Ireland. Her collection of hydrangeas that flower from June to November is approved by the Conservatoire des Collections Végétales Spécialisées (Conservatory of Specialized Plant Collections).

PARC FLORAL WILLIAM FARCY
76550 Offranville
Tel: + 33 (0)2 35 85 40 42
As well as the hundred-year-old tree that guards the eighteenth-century church, the site abounds in rose bushes, cypresses, magnolias, azaleas, tulips, and camellias, arranged in a maze of twelve themed gardens.

PARC NATUREL REGIONAL DES BOUCLES DE LA SEINE NORMANDE
76940 Notre Dame de Bliquetuit
Tel: + 33 (0)2 35 37 23 16

The park is found just near the Pont de Brotonne and crosses a number of communes that are linked by roads (*routes*) with symbolic names: Route des Chaumières (thatch-roofed cottages), Route des Fruits (fruits), Route du Blé au Pain (bread wheat). For a picturesque cultural activity, cycle or drive through, stopping at abbeys and museums presenting professions of yesteryear and regional products.

CHÂTEAUX

CHÂTEAU DE CANY-BARVILLE
76450 Cany-Barville
Tel: + 33 (0)2 35 97 87 36
With its alleys shaded by oak trees, its arched doors, and its windows with mullions, this sixteenth-century residence is an imposing stone and brick building, at the feet of which the Durdent river flows peacefully. Faithful to the great classical tradition, two lateral wings frame the main building. Less traditional is the double staircase in the form of a horseshoe (perhaps intended as a good luck sign) that gives a certain lyricism to the whole, especially to the large courtyard with asymmetrical pavilions. On the first floor, the large green salon is an ideal showroom for its Regency wood objects. On the second floor, the walls are covered with tapestries from Flanders. The kitchen brings us back down to earth with a whole range of period utensils, stoves, and crockery. Open for visits in July and August only.

CHÂTEAU DE FILIERES

Gommerville près du Havre
76430 Saint-Romain de Colbosc
Tel: + 33 (0)2 35 20 53 30
Inside, Oriental touches grace the rooms decorated with porcelains and hangings from the Far East, Sèvres biscuit medallions with royal effigies, and prestigious furniture. Visible from the road after you pass Gommerville, the château stands proudly with its façade composed of white stones from Caen. Its left wing dates from the sixteenth century, while its right wing was built in the eighteenth century. The courtyard is surrounded by a moat. In the park on the left of the residence, stands the "beech tree cathedral" —seven rows of trees whose roots and branches bend together into the shape of a basilica vault.

CURIOSITIES

LIBRAIRIE LE CHAT PITRE

Claire Lamotte, 1, quai Berigny
76400 Fécamp
Tel: + 33 (0)2 35 10 12 54
A gorgeous little bookshop on the quay of the port, an animated part of the town. A place to find gifts, with an excellent selection of illustrated books on the region.

EURE

HOTELS

CHÂTEAU LA THILLAYE

27450 Saint Christophe-sur-Condé
Tel: + 33 (0)2 32 56 07 24
Fax: + 33 (0)2 32 56 70 47
www.chateaulathillaye.com
Constructed in 1645, this château with a brick façade and varnished cross braces is found five miles (8 km) from Pont Audemer, not far from the fashionable resort towns. Present owners Roxane Longpré and Patrick Matton reserve a warm welcome for guests in this hotel that offers a music salon, a library and an eighteenth-century common room. The five elegantly decorated guest rooms all overlook the seventy acre (28 ha) park, where it is possible to participate in numerous outdoor activities.

BED-AND-BREAKFASTS

ABBAYE NOTRE-DAME DU BEC

27800 Le Bec-Helllouin
Tel: + 33 (0)2 32 43 72 62
Email: accueil@abbayedubec.com

The knight Hellouin founded this abbey in 1034 in the Vallée de la Risle, next to Le Bec river. Today, this Benedictine abbey still offers accommodation to visitors in search of a place to rest and contemplate.

MOULIN DE CONNELLES

40, route d'Amfreville-sous-les-Monts
27430 Connelles
Tel: + 33 (0)2 32 59 53 33
Situated on the banks of the Seine, this Anglo-Norman manor with Belle Epoque décor is part of the Châteaux et Hôtels de France group. A seven and a half acre (3 ha) park surrounds the residence. It is possible to take romantic boat rides on the Seine here.

LE PHARE

27210 Fatouville-Gestrain,
Tel: + 33 (0)2 32 57 66 56
Anne and Jean-François Durand
Rather than receiving guests in the lighthouse bought by Mme Durand's great-grandfather, the current owner and her husband dispose of five pretty bedrooms in the former watchman's house, with décor by inspired the elements. From the top of the one-hundred-foot-high (32 m) lighthouse constructed in 1850, the view of the countryside and the Seine is unbeatable.

LE PRESSOIR DU MONT

Hameau le Mont, 27210 Saint-Maclou
Tel: + 33 (0)2 32 41 42 55
Close to Deauville and Pont-Audemer, an ancient winepress with a thatched roof offers bucolically decked-out rooms right in the middle of the Norman countryside.

RESTAURANTS AND BISTROS

LE BOUCHE A OREILLES

3, rue Jules Ferry, 27170 Beaumont Le Roger
Tel: + 33 (0)2 32 45 57 27
A pleasant bistro decorated with bric-a-brac items, that hosts concerts and theme nights.
(see photo page 178)

LE VIEUX PUIT

6, rue Notre-dame du Pré, 27500 Pont Audemer
Tel.: + 33 (0)2 32 41 01 48
A splendid seventeenth-century timber-framed house traditionally decorated with copperware and ceramics. Well known and authentic.

LE MOULIN DES FOURGES

38, rue du Moulin, 27630 Fourges
Tel: + 33 (0)2 32 52 12 12

A magnificent residence with timber frames and stone walls in the middle of the countryside, by the Epte river. In summer, enjoy a lunch of regional products on the riverbank; in winter, linger over dinner by the open fire. A rustic and elegant place, ideal for family weekends, where you can take shelter in a haven of peace found at the heart of the region's tourist and cultural attractions.

ANCIEN HOTEL BAUDY

81, rue Claude Monet, 27620 Giverny
Tel: + 33 (0)2 32 21 10 03
This was the first artists' meeting spot established at the time when Claude Monet lived in Giverny and numerous American painters passed through. Metcalf, the first such transatlantic client, stayed here in 1886. Then came Robinson, Butler, Marie Cassatt, Frieske, Sargent … all were quickly seduced by this place conducive to rest and inspiration, not far from the world's most famous Impressionist garden. Today, the hotel has restored a little workshop where painting schools regularly conduct classes, and its sloped grounds boast a rose garden with heady perfumes. To set off the pictorial theme of the place, the dining room where delicious mixed salads are served has walls covered with paintings.

ARTISANS

WEATHERVANE CRAFTSMAN

Jean-Pierre Masquelier,
La Canarderie, 27160 Francheville
Tel: + 33 (0)2 32 32 62 76
A beautiful selection of over fifty zinc weathervanes is displayed by the artisan in a little workshop set up in his home.

EPIS DE FAITAGE (FINIALS)

Pimont-couverture, Z.A. La Baudrière – B.P. 29
27520 Bourgtheroulde
Tel: + 33 (0)2 35 77 47 80
Specializing in roof framework and covering, the company also makes lead and copper finials by request. It has no boutique to receive clients, but catalogs are available.

SMALL MUSEUMS

CHÂTEAU DE BIZY

Avenue des Capucins, 27200 Vernon
Tel: + 33 (0)2 32 51 00 82
A large classical residence with colonnades on its façade that lend it the feel of a Louisiana cotton plantation house. The more austere

southern façade faces a courtyard whose limits are marked by stables now used as garages for vintage cars. The château has some magnificent touches: Versailles wood flooring, inlaid furniture, a staircase sculpted from oak, Regency wood objects, and eighteenth-century tapestries. Illustrious guests have stayed here, including Napoleon Bonaparte, Marshals Suchet, Massena and Davout, the Duke of Penthièvre, General Le Suire, King Louis Philippe, and Baron Schickler. Today the Albufera family owns this residence that Coutant d'Ivry constructed in 1740 for the Duc de Belle-Isle, who was Marshal of France and grandson of Fouquet.

MUSEE D'ART AMERICAIN

99, rue Claude Monet , 27620 Giverny
Tel: + 33 (0)2 32 51 94 65
Situated near the residence of Impressionist painter Claude Monet, it houses the works of American artists including John Sargent and Lilla Cabot Perrit, who lived in Giverny, seduced by the magic of the place.

MUSEE JULES MICHELET

Château de Vascoeuil, rue Michelet
27910 Vascoeuil
Tel: + 33 (0)2 35 23 62 35
Surrounded by small valleys and a park, this château was once a haughty feudal residence featuring a tower, a beautiful oak-framed dovecote, and thick walls. Historian Jules Michelet made this stone building, situated right next to Rouen, into a place of rest and meditation. Every morning, Michelet would climb up to the turret, where, perched up high, he worked on his manuscripts, notably the prestigious *History of France*.

PARKS AND GARDENS

ARBORETUM D'HARCOURT

27800 Harcourt
Tel: + 33 (0)2 32 46 29 70
This arboretum stretches out over one thousand acres (400 ha). At its threshold stand two majestic Lebanese cedars, one hundred feet (30 m) high and two hundred years old. Created in 1802, the space is made up of four hundred species of rare trees from all around the world: spruces, willows, cedars, oaks, and conifers. The forest surrounding the arboretum is equally abundant in wonders from the ends of the earth—Polish larches, Chilean beech trees, Caucasian pine trees, and American sequoias, to name just a few.

CHÂTEAU DE BEAUMESNIL

27410 Beaumesnil
Tel: + 33 (0)2 32 44 40 09
Constructed between 1633 and 1640, this château—one of the most beautiful in Normandy—was mentioned as "le Mesnil royal" by writer Jean de la Varende in his novel *Nez de Cuir*. Today, it houses the Furstenberg-Beaumesnil foundation, whose mission it is to restore this beautiful relic of the past. Inside, extravagance reigns: period furniture, an airy staircase, a library and a bookbinding museum. Outside, the brick and stone façade beautifully sets off the famous labyrinth of box-trees and the pond reflecting the château's image. (see photos pages 66–67)

CHÂTEAU DE VANDRIMARE

27382 Vandrimare
Tel: + 33 (0)2 32 49 03 57
Its labyrinth is an ideal place for daydreaming. The rest of the park is arranged in themes drawn from the senses and the essence of life itself. The water garden with its lakeside plants, the garden of touch, the cloister garden dedicated to things spiritual, the berry garden that pays tribute to the sense of taste … these gardens all deliver clear messages. Wisteria, vines, and rose bushes further add to the mysticism of the place. In the center of the estate is a space made up of slow-growing and powerfully-perfumed plants—sage, rosemary, mint, chamomile, oregano, thyme … their presence suggests an attempt to counter the passing of time. To confirm the philosophy of the place, the colors of flowers and the texture of vegetation follow the relentless waltz of the seasons.

FONDATION CLAUDE MONET

84, rue Claude Monet
27620 Giverny
Tel: + 33 (0)2 32 51 28 21
Gérald van der Kamp currently manages this foundation which finances the restoration of the house bequeathed to the State in 1966. (see photos pages 74–77)

MOULIN D'ANDE

Centre culturel et artistique
27430 Andé
Tel: + 33 (0)2 32 59 90 89
Cultural and artistic center
Film directors Louis Malle and Robert Enrico stopped by here. Singer-composer Barbara also wrote a few songs here. The site was constructed in 1197. A few centuries later, in 1957, musician and arts patron Suzanne

Lipinska inherited the place, did it up, restored the orange grove, and made it into an artists' residence. Lipinska conceived the place as an old-fashioned literary and musical salon. Concerts and dinners are regularly organized to present the artists who stay here. The residence also has a few bed-and-breakfast rooms available by booking only.

CHÂTEAUX

CHÂTEAU DU CHAMP DE BATAILLE

27110 Le Neubourg
Tel: + 33 (0)2 32 34 84 34
In the seventeenth century, Alexandre de Créqui constructed this château that would become, during WWII, an asylum, prisoner camp and women's prison. The Duke of Harcourt bought the property in 1947 and began renovations that were later taken over by the famous Parisian decorator Jacques Garcia. The latter is responsible for the site's magnificent old-fashioned touches, with extravagant gardens and refurbished interiors. Worth seeing are the Palladian hall, the billiards room whose walls are covered with sixteenth-century tapestries from Brussels representing the signs of the zodiac, the marble salon, and the Beuvron salon decorated with Egyptian-style furniture.

ORNE

HOTELS

LE MANOIR DU LYS

Route de Juvigny – La Croix Gautier
61140 Bagnoles-de-l'Orne
Tel: + 33 (0)2 33 37 80 69,
www.manoir-du-lys.fr
The hotel offers elegant rooms, but those wishing for more space have another option: wooden pavilions on stilts in the forest clearing, with a terrace, living room, bedroom, and large bathroom.

BED-AND-BREAKFASTS

ABBAYE DE LA TRAPPE

61380 Soligny-la-Trappe
Tel: + 33 (0)2 33 84 17 05
Email: la.trappe@wanadoo.fr
Located in the south of L'Aigle, this is one of the most famous Cistercian abbeys in Le Perche and in France. In the seventeenth century,

Abbot Armand de Rancé restored the site and created a strict monastic order based on silence. This abbey offers accommodation and a beautiful, peaceful environment to all seeking silence and rest.

CHÂTEAU DE LA GRANDE NOË

61290 Longny-au-Perche
Tel: + 33 (0)2 33 73 63 30
Email: grandenoe@wanadoo.fr
Pascale and Jacques de Longcamp Moulicent
Between Verneuil and Mortagne, this eighteenth-century château stands proudly in the middle of a large park. Pascale and Jacques de Longcamp Moulicent are owners of this residence which has preserved its original furnishings. Each of the three bedrooms has a view of the park.

MANOIR DE LORMARIN

La maison du fournil (The bake-house)
Route de Dance, 61340 Nocé
Tel: + 33 (0)2 33 25 41 89
A pretty medieval manor house with a monastic-style interior. (see photos pages 168–169, 191)

L'ORANGERIE

9, rue des Prés, 61290 Longny-au-Perche
Tel, home: + 33 (0)2 33 25 11 78
Tel, office: + 33 (0)2 33 73 67 19
Email: desailly-fondeur@tele2.fr
In the Orne, all seasons have their own distinct charm. Winter offers sleepy landscapes and hunts for game, spring allows walks in the forest, summer is pleasant for waterside strolls, autumn is delightful for its roast chestnuts, pan-fried mushrooms, and evenings around a fireplace. Edith and Marc Desailly have made L'Orangerie in the heart of the Parc Naturel du Perche a superb guest house. Here, bedrooms are lyrically decorated in rustic themes, and in the kitchen, the host concocts delicious regional specialties. The wash-house has been transformed into a pond where goldfish swim and ducks splash.

LA REVARDIERE

Isabelle and Jean-François Chanteur
61400 Feings
Tel: + 33 (0)2 33 73 88 64
email: isabelle.chanteur@wanadoo.fr
An unpretentious welcome awaits guests in this ancient farm perched on top of a hill near Remalard, in the middle of the countryside. The two soberly decorated bedrooms offer guests absolute tranquility.

RESTAURANTS AND BISTROS

LA MAISON D'HORBE

Cafe, tearoom, brookshop, and antiques
Grande rue, 61360 La Perrière
Tel: + 33 (0)2 33 73 18 41
The tearoom, also a bookshop crammed with contemporary novels and illustrated books on the region, has become a veritable literary meeting place. A pleasant spot to chat over unusually flavored teas accompanied with cakes and homemade jams. (see photo page 180)

ARTISANS

ATELIER DE FORGE BOUVET

Rue des Sports – BP 23, 61100 Flers
Tel: + 33 (0)2 33 98 40 00
This decorative ironwork workshop specializes in door handles and furniture in brass, stainless steel and cast steel. Attractively finished handcrafted creations produced using old-fashioned techniques.

SMALL MUSEUMS

CHÂTEAU MARTIN DU GARD

Le Tertre 61130 Sérigny
Tel: + 33 (0)2 33 73 18 30
Visits by appointment only.
The house remains in its original state.
1937 Nobel Prize winner Roger Martin du Gard made his dwelling into a place dedicated to the arts and literature. After its glory days, the estate fell into a dark period, particularly after the death of the writer's wife Hélène in 1949. The place came to life again during a final golden period when writers André Malraux, Albert Camus, and Jean Delay stayed occasionally to prevent their host from falling into depression. Today, the writer's granddaughter Anne-Véronique de Coppet maintains the place and its memories.

HARAS DU PIN

61310 Le Pin-au-Haras
Tel: + 33 (0)2 33 36 68 68,
Fax: + 33 (0)2 33 35 57 70
Email: meneux@voila.fr
The most famous stud farm in France and perhaps Europe. Mansart drew up the plans, Le Notre designed the garden. The farm was finished in 1730 and is surrounded by a domain measuring 3,000 acres (1,200 ha). It represents the finest in breeding, competition, and

preparation for the most prestigious equestrian events. Nearly half of all French trotters are raised in this region. (see photos pages 46–47)

MUSEE DES BEAUX ARTS ET DE LA DENTELLE

Cour Carrée de la Dentelle
12 rue du Capitaine Charles Aveline
61000 Alençon
Tel: + 33 (0)2 33 32 40 07
In 1665, Colbert, a minister under Louis XIV, turned needle lace (*la dentelle*) into a real industry. It was thanks to Madame de la Perrière, a specialist in Venetian lace, that Alençon lace and French lace were developed. While this craft may now seem somewhat old-fashioned, it nevertheless remains an art form that incites passion among its enthusiasts. Today, most workshops are found in monasteries. This museum exhibits true treasures of delicacy and finesse.

MUSEE DE LA DAME AUX CAMELIAS

Château de Gacé
61230 Gacé
Tel: + 33 (0)2 33 35 50 24
Jean-Marie Choulet, the museum creator with a passionate interest in the life of Marie Duplessis, will personally reply to any questions you may have on the most famous courtesan of the nineteenth century. Objects and souvenirs on the three floors of the museum present the life of the young woman with a tragic and brilliant destiny. A slideshow illustrates the major stages of her very short life. (see photo page 198)

MUSEE DE L'EPICERIE ET DES COMMERCES D'AUTREFOIS

61190 Lignerolles
Tel: + 33 (0)2 33 25 91 07
A picturesque setting for twenty thousand objects that bear the poetic stamp of the small shops of yesteryear. Ex-supermarket manager Pierre Marzorati converted this ten-room former guest house into a museum that he filled with items from his personal collections. His first piece was a painted metal plaque that sang the praises of plant-based shoe polish. (see photo page 199)

MAISON DES DENTELLES ET DU POINT D'ARGENTAN

34 rue de la Noë
61200 Argentan
Tel: + 33 (0)2 33 67 40 56
Argentan lace is woven in the cloisters and workshops of a Benedictine abbey. The motif resembling the cells of a beehive was created

in the eighteenth century. In this art, machines have no place: lace is handmade according to tips passed on from one lace-maker to another. To make this craft all the more mysterious, each lace-maker is privy only to the secrets of his or her own stitch, and knows nothing of the stitches of workshop colleagues. The museum exhibits collars, handkerchiefs, chains, tablecloths, and doilies.

PARKS AND GARDENS

CHÂTEAU DE SASSY

61570 Saint-Christophe-le-Jajolet
Tel: + 33 (0)2 33 35 32 66
Magnificent terraces descend to the gardens *à la Française*, with an elegant eighteenth-century residence in the background. (see photos pages 70–71)

JARDIN FRANÇOIS LE CLOS

61340 Préaux-du-Perche
Tel: + 33 (0)2 37 49 64 19
A modern-day garden that brings together all genres of landscapes, plant collections, and architectural designs. The site also includes a farm, an open-air amphitheater and an orange grove. Open from sunrise to sunset. (see photo page 90)

LES JARDINS DU MANOIR DE PONTGIRARD

61290 Monceaux
Tel: + 33 (0)2 33 73 61 49
The manor dating back to the sixteenth century is found in the middle of a garden. The latter is made up of terraces whose limits are marked by topiaries. Fountains, wells, marsh, cypress spurges, themed collections, a pergola, cascading water stairs, and a herb garden are some of the features of this magnificent floral space in Le Perche. A terrace with the fountain of Plato has a view over the wall-enclosed garden.

JARDINS DE LA PETITE-ROCHELLE

Mme d'Andlau
La Petite Rochelle, 61110 Rémalard
Tel: + 33 (0)2 33 73 85 38
This pretty botanical garden covering two and a half acres (1 ha) is made up of flowers, bushes, trees, and water holes. September is a particularly good time to visit as the esters are in bloom. The garden is unfortunately closed in summer. Open only for guided group tours, it is necessary to telephone Madame d'Andlau, the creator of these grounds, before visiting.

LE PRIEURE SAINT-MICHEL

61120 Crouttes-Vimoutiers
Tel: + 33 (0)2 33 39 15 15
In this medieval priory that was once a dependency of the Abbaye de Jumièges, the garden is an absolute delight. It includes a rose garden, an orchard, an enclosure with bushes, herbs, irises and medicinal plants (a place to heal the body and spirit), and finally, a little water-lily-topped pond where the water is renewed by a spring. (see photo page 85)

ANTIQUE DEALERS

LA MAISON FASSIER

Antiquaire
55 rue de l'Eglise
61110 Remalard
Tel.: + 33 (0)2 33 73 56 21
or 33 (0)6 07 34 36 72
Email: lamaisonfassier@aol.com
Claude offers household linen and fabrics, antique or reworked with synthetic fur, fiber fleece, linen or hemp. Her husband Alain sells unusual knickknacks and sumptuous antique wood objects. An elegant and unique universe where these two lovers of objects from yesterday and today have invested their souls and their passion. (see photo page 191)

LE MOULIN DE LA PLEUGERE

Secondhand dealer and guest house
61380 Soligny-la-Trappe
Tel: + 33 (0)2 33 34 33 36
The small secondhand shop, not far from the windmill, sells poetic and sentimental objects that exude a delicate rustic sensibility. (see photos pages 170, 191)

LA MAISON DE TARA

Anne-Marie Mesnil
Dealer in antiques and secondhand wares
1, rue du Perche,
61110 Boissy-Maugis
Tel: + 33 (0)2 33 83 54 98
A splendid collection of objects from the past and creations from today, presented in a very attractive setting by an ex-media officer from Paris.

CHÂTEAUX

CHÂTEAU DE CARROUGES

61320 Carrouges
Tel: + 33 (0)2 33 27 20 32
The château is situated a little way downwards from the village. Its entrance pavilion was

constructed in the fourteenth century, but the residence was renovated several times. The fortress, once surrounded by a moat, has been turned into a classically beautiful residence. From its medieval past, only the dungeon remains. In the 1930s, the domain was purchased by the State and made into the headquarters of the Normandy-Maine Regional Natural Park. The latter organizes exhibitions on flora, fauna, local crafts, and professions from the past.

CALVADOS

HOTELS

L'ABSINTHE

1, rue de la Ville, 14600 Honfleur
Tel: + 33 (0)2 31 89 23 23
Email: reservation@absinthe.fr
Despite its name, which is associated with a state of drunkenness, this small charming hotel with modern rooms is a hearth of calm, thanks to its location in a former presbytery close to the old fort.

CHÂTEAU D'AUDRIEU

14250 Audrieu
Tel: + 33 (0)2 31 80 21 52
www.chateaudaudrieu.com
Email: audrieu@relaischateaux.com
Owned by the same family since it came into existence, this eighteenth-century estate is found in a one-hundred acre (40 ha) park twelve miles (20 km) from the sea. Light and nature are displayed to advantage in this hotel decorated in period furniture. Graced with a magnificent courtyard, the château is classified as a historic monument, and moreover, is a good base for excursions in the area, for example to the D-Day beaches.

CHÂTEAU DE GOVILLE

14330 Le-Breuil-en-Bessin
Tel: + 33 (0)2 31 22 19 28
Email: chateaugoville@wanadoo.fr
A magnificent family residence decked out with antique furniture and doll's houses that reveal the distinct taste of those who have lived here for several generations. Each bedroom carries on its door the name of the family ancestor it is named after. The elegance continues in the dining room where candlelight brings beautiful reflections out of the crystal accessories. The menu has an excellent selection of regional specialties, such as shrimp flame-grilled with *calvados* and Bayeux-style chicken.

LA CHAUMIERE

Route du Littoral, 14600 Honfleur
Tel: + 33 (0)2 31 81 63 20
Email: chaumiere@relaischateaux.com
On the edge of Honfleur, on the road to
Trouville, this hotel in an old seventeenth-
century farmhouse stands by the sea.
Seeking to offer clients peace and tranquility,
only a few rooms (each with a view of the
garden) are available. One suite has a view
of the sea.

FERME SAINT-SIMEON

Rue Adolphe Marais, 14600 Honfleur
Tel: + 33 (0)2 31 81 78 00
This very luxurious Relais & Château
establishment has a park overlooking the
estuary of the Seine. It was once a guest house
run by the legendary Madame Toutain where
Impressionist painters liked to meet. (see photo
page 156)

HOTEL DES LOGES

18, rue Brûlée, 14600 Honfleur
Tel: + 33 (0)2 31 89 38 26
With its succession of modern rooms opening
onto extremely calm courtyards in the midst of
the tourist buzz, this hotel has opted for a much
appreciated simplicity. Opposite the hotel,
owner Catherine Chouridis has opened a small
boutique where furniture and room decorations
are available, making for original souvenirs of
the weekend away.

HOTEL DU GOLF

Le Mont Canisy, Saint-Arnoult
14803 Deauville
Tel: + 33 (0)2 31 14 24 00
Email: hoteldugolfdeauville@lucienbarriere.com
About a mile (2 km) from the town center, here
are 20,000 square feet (2,000m²) of Art Déco
encircled by a grass lawn. From the rotunda,
the sunsets are as beautiful as those from the
islands. The hotel has a bar, "Le Green,"
a restaurant, "La Pommeraie," a swimming
pool and exercise space, and above all,
a magnificent golf course.

HOTEL NORMANDY

38 rue Jean Mermoz, 14800 Deauville
Tel: + 33 (0)2 31 14 39 59
Email: normandy@lucienbarriere.com
A timber-framed manor right in the center of
town, facing the sea, not far from the casino.
Offers the classic four-star luxury of this
famous vacation destination. (see photo
page 154)

HOTEL ROYAL

Boulevard Cornuché, 14804 Deauville
Tel: + 33 (0)2 31 98 66 33
Email: royal@lucienbarriere.com
The town's other grand hotel, with a typically
Norman neoclassical checkerboard façade.
The hotel overlooks the ocean.

LA MAISON DE LUCIE

44, rue des Capucins, 14600 Honfleur
Tel: + 33 (0)2 31 14 40 40
Email: info@lamaisondelucie.com
In a peaceful little road, this beautiful
eighteenth-century house opens out onto an
enclosed patio. Some rooms—the number four,
for instance—have a view of the estuary.
Available in a little brick building is a suite with
refined, unpretentious décor—perfect for a
dream weekend.

LES MAISONS DE LEA

Place Sainte-Catherine, 14600 Honfleur
Tel: + 33 (0)2 31 14 49 49
Email: contact@lesmaisonsdelea.com
Four houses make up this elegant vine-
covered construction found on the square in
the town center, right near the magnificent
historic marketplace. Each is named
according to its unique features. La Maison
Romance has a very British atmosphere,
La Maison du Capitaine ("captain") has a
marine flavor, La Maison de Campagne
("country") has a rustic feel, and La Maison
Baltimore draws inspiration from the east
coast of the United States.

MANOIR DE PLACY

Placy, 14570 Clécy
Tel: + 33 (0)2 31 59 20 00
The house is covered with vines, the bedrooms
are simple and tastefully decorated. The manor
is in fact a dependency of the Moulin de Vey,
and while it may be less ornate and less
imposing than the latter, it is no less charming.
Service is very friendly, and the place is
recommended for the beautiful sound of silence
it offers.

LE SAINT JAMES

16, rue de la plage
14360 Trouville-sur-Mer
Tel: + 33 (0)2 31 88 05 23
An elegant three-star seaside hotel with antique
furniture and a lounge where an open fire
crackles in winter. A refined and discreet
address oozing with the town's classy beach
resort atmosphere.

BED-AND-BREAKFASTS

CHÂTEAU DE DRAMARD

Chemin Dramard, 14510 Houlgate
Tel: + 33 (0)2.31.24.63.41
Email: dramard@worldonline.fr
Surrounded by trees, the château stands in the
middle of a park and an English lawn. Inside,
the tone is refined, with period furniture,
embroidered tablecloths, and fine tableware.
Here, the rooms—or rather suites—all have
their own living room and, of course, their own
elegant bathroom.

LE COTIL

Mecki Dauré, Route de Falaise
14140 Le Mesnil-Simon
Tel: + 33 (0)2 31 31 47 86
Email: mecki.daure@wanadoo.fr
You will find this seventeenth-century timber-
framed house in the land of stud farms and
manors, in the middle of apple trees and
fields where cows doze and chew cud.
Outside of Lisieux, this property lies beside a
river, near natural grottoes. Inside, the décor
is eye-catching: antique objects, carpets, kilim
cushions and painted furniture. The latter is
painted by the owner in the workshop on the
ground floor.

LA COUR L'ÉPEE

14340 Saint Aubin Lebizay
Tel: + 33 (0)2.31.65.13.45
Email: aj.tesniere@wanadoo.fr
Nine miles (14km) from Cabourg, you will find
this house that exudes old-fashioned charm in
the middle of a lovely flower garden.

LA COUR SAINTE-CATHERINE

74, rue du Puits
14600 Honfleur
Tel: + 33 (0)2 31 89 42 40
Monsieur and Madame Giaglis
In old Honfleur, close to the Eglise Sainte-
Catherine and the port, but far from the
tourist strip, Monsieur and Madame Giaglis
have renovated the buildings of a
seventeenth-century convent, and
transformed them into fishermen's cottages.
The bedrooms are decorated with
secondhand furniture placed on sea-grass
rush matting that reminds guests of the
proximity of the water. Windows overlook a
garden of mystical flowers that embalm this
slightly spiritual place with their perfumes.
Breakfast is served in a little dining room
or on the wooden terrace.

LE COURTILLAGE

14320 Clinchamps-sur-Orne
Tel: + 33 (0)2 31 23 87 63
Seven miles (12 km) south of the town, Annick
Hervieu and Paul Masson have set up this
nineteenth-century house full of hidden stairs
and corners, books and antique crockery. A
cosy and romantic atmosphere heightened by
quaint details. The name of a writer or the title
of a famous novel—for instance Beaumarchais
(author of The Marriage of Figaro)—graces the
door of each guest room.

DOMAINE DE LA PICQUOTERIE

Tel: + 33 (0)2 31 92 09 82
Seven enclosures of greenery make up the park
surrounding an old fortified farm not far from
Bayeux. Features perennial plants, hellebores,
a rose garden, and a garden à la Française.

LA FERME DE LA POMME

14590 Le Pin
Tel: + 33 (0)6 61 45 45 68
Jocelyne Sylla
This restored seventeenth-century farm, found
opposite the famous stud farm, only has a few
rooms available, but this address is noteworthy
for its distinct Norman features: a romantic
décor with fireplaces, painted wooden beams,
timber frames, cobblestones, antique furniture,
veils and broderies anglaises, not to mention
the fine jams and cakes that Jocelyne Sylla
cooks with motherly devotion. The tempting
aromas created by her afternoon baking
sessions are the very stuff of childhood
memories.

LA FERME DU LIEU-BOURG

Chemin de la Haute-Rue
14950 Saint-Pierre-Azif
Tel: + 33 (0)2 31 39 64 90
An eighteenth-century farmhouse found in a
very peaceful rural spot surrounded by fields
and a flower garden. Only two bedrooms are
available, both with fabric-covered walls. There
are unfortunately no restaurant facilities, but
delicious breakfasts are served in the beautiful
common room furnished with period pieces.

LA FERME DES POIRIERS ROSES

Saint Philibert des Champs, 14130 Pont l'Evêque
Tel: + 33 (0)2 31 64 72 14
In a timber-framed farm typical of the Pays
d'Auge. Plant lovers will adore this place, for
its bedrooms and living room (where delicious
breakfasts are served) abound in fresh and
dried flowers.

LA MAISON DE SOPHIE
Lieu Goguet, 14950 Saint-Etienne-la-Thillaye
Tel: + 33 (0)2 31 65 69 98
Three miles (5 km) from Pont-l'Evêque, this former presbytery is a haven of peace, with fireside dinners, gourmet breakfasts, and cooking lessons. Cozy and unpretentious. (see photo page 162)

MANOIR DE CREPON
Route de Bazenville, 14480 Crépon
Tel: + 33 (0)2 31 22 21 27
A charming residence dating back to the seventeenth century, with an elegant brick façade, two and a half miles (4 km) from the sea. Overlooking the grounds where hundred-year-old trees are planted, the bedrooms are tastefully decorated with a delicious aroma of the past (property owner Madame Poisson is also an antique collector). Breakfasts are served in the dining room converted from the manor's former kitchen, where stunning log fires burn in winter.

MANOIR DU CHAMP VERSAN
Chemin du Champ Versan, 14340 Bonnebosq
Tel: + 33 (0)2 31 65 11 07
A magnificent country manor house, rustic yet refined, surrounded by fields where horses, cows and chickens roam! A strong rural flavor. (see photos pages 158–159)

LES MILLE FEUILLES
A LA CAMPAGNE
Domaine de la Petite Lande, 14290 Cerqueux
Tel: + 33 (0)2 31 63 89 77
Near Orbec, in the heart of the Pays d'Auge, stands this domain where clients of Pierre Brinon—creator of the stunning Parisian flower shop Mille Feuilles—enjoy meeting by the fireplace in artistically decorated salons. The bedrooms are named after the magnificent trees that can be seen from the windows: *le hêtre* (beech tree), *le marronnier* (chestnut tree), *le pommier* (apple tree), *le saule* (willow tree). The color scheme and the collection of objects, furniture, and statues make for an astonishing interior. Food connoisseurs will also enjoy stopping here, for Pierre Brinon is a passionate cook: the evening meals are delectable, and the perfume of oven-fresh brioches accompanies breakfast served in the large kitchen. (see photos pages 160–161)

LE REPOS DES CHINEURS
Chemin de l'Eglise
14340 Notre-Dame-d'Estrées
Tel: + 33 (0)2 31 63 72 51

A former coaching house on the cider route, transformed into a charming residence and tearoom. The adjoining secondhand shop offers rustic crockery, English furniture, and loom armchairs. The bedrooms overlooking the garden are quieter than those overlooking the road.

LA TERRASSE DE L'ESTUAIRE
Vasouy, 14600 Honfleur
Tel: + 33 (0)2 31 88 76 85
Email: contact@laterrassedelestuaire.com
Madame Mélanie N'ze
Formerly called "Les Pavillons," these constructions came into being in the seventeenth century. The two independent buildings are separated by a large terrace. All the rooms have a view of the sea. Found in the gentle Pays d'Auge, two miles (3.5 km) from the center of Honfleur and on the road to Deauville, they have the advantage of a lush green setting and a panoramic view of the Baie de Seine.

RESTAURANTS AND BISTROS

L'AUBERGE DE L'AIGLE D'OR
68, rue de Vaucelles
14130 Pont l'Evêque
Tel: + 33 (0)2 31 6 5 05 25
A former coaching house dating back to the sixteenth century, now an unbeatable gastronomic stop in the Pays d'Auge where food connoisseurs will delight in excellent cooking, both innovative and 100 percent Norman—for example, chicken breasts cooked in traditional Pays d'Auge style followed by a cheese platter and green apple sorbet with Calvados.

AUBERGE DES DEUX TONNEAUX
Pierrefite-en-Auge
14130 Pont-l'Évêque
Tel: + 33 (0)2 31 64 09 31
This roadside country café with a thatched roof is the perfect example of the little Norman inn. (see photo page 177)

BRASSERIE LES VAPEURS
160, quai Fernand-Moureaux
14360 Trouville-sur-Mer,
Tel: + 33 (0)2 31 88 15 24
A real institution, created in 1927, now managed by Martine and Gérard Bazire. A simple and popular brasserie-bistro where it is the done thing to have one's regular table. The place is famous for its décor—yellow walls, neon lights, posters—and above all, for its specialties:

moules marinières, mussels cooked in white wine with or without cream; steamed shrimp; baskets of oysters from Saint-Vaast-la-Hougue; fish soup; and to end on a high note, *tarte Tatin*.

CAFE GONDREE
Pegasus Bridge, 14860 Ranville
A little café and museum on the Canal de l'Orne. Picturesque and rich in history. (see photos pages 175)

CHEZ LE BOUGNAT
25 bis, rue Gaston Manneville
14160 Dives-sur-Mer, Tel: + 33 (0)2 31 91 06 13
A former hardware shop that offers delicious dishes concocted from regional products. (see photo page 174)

CHEZ MIOCQUE
81, rue Eugène Colas, 14800 Deauville
Tel: + 33 (0)2 31 88 09 52
All Deauville inhabitants agree: this is the best and most pleasant place to eat in the town, with its Parisian décor and its walls covered with photos of celebrities who are regulars here. Also renowned for its eclectic menu.

LA DIGUE
Avenue de la République
14640 Villers-sur-Mer
Tel: + 33 (0)2 31 88 61 47
One of the good restaurants in this town known for its holiday activities, concerts, casino, and strolls along rivers or on the cliff tops of the Vaches Noires.

HOSTELLERIE GUILLAUME
LE CONQUERANT
Rue d'Hastings, 14160 Dives sur Mer
Tel: + 33 (0)2 31 91 07 26
This historically rich inn came into existence in the sixteenth century. Madame de Sévigné stayed here at the end of the following century, then Impressionist painter Eugène Boudin, writer Alexandre Dumas, and Winston Churchill—just a few names that indicate the heights of fame reached by this former coaching house. Today, it is a very elegant hotel whose beauty is set off by the courtyard and outbuildings. The restaurant provides a sophisticated setting for the refined specialties it offers.

LE PAVE D'AUGE
Place du village, Beuvron-en-Auge
14430 Dozulé
Tel: + 33 (0)2 31 79 26 71

Fireplace, wooden beams, wood flooring, tablecloths and bouquets of flowers ... this restaurant is a warm and down-to-earth place to dine. Chef Odile Engel picks produce from the market herself. Among her delicious creations are John Dory filets with butter and fresh tomato, oysters in cider, and of course, her famous chicken from the Vallée d'Auge, all prepared with regional products and traditional utensils. Here, simplicity reigns to produce excellent-value meals.

LE POT D'ETAIN
Sur la route de Caen, 14340 Manerbe
Tel: + 33 (0)2 31 61 00 64
A picturesque place to eat in this village reputed for its fifteenth-century church in a gorgeous hilly setting.

LES QUATRE CHATS
8, rue d'Orléans, 14360 Trouville-sur-mer
Tel: + 33 (0)2 31 88 94 94
The town's trendy bohemian spot. Former barman of the Closerie des Lilas in Paris, Serge Salmon and his wife Muriel offer original dishes in their bistro decorated with a metro seat. Clients are fashionable, Parisian, and often well known.

GOURMET STORES

À L'ÉPI D'OR
Boulangerie, 28, rue du Général Leclerc
14510 Houlgate
Tel: + 33 (0)2 31 24 80 94
Opposite the market place, this traditional cake shop and bakery concocts delectable Norman soufflés and regional specialties.

À CHARLOTTE CORDAY
Pâtisserie, 172, bd Fernand Moureaux
14360 Trouville-sur-mer
Tel: + 33 (0)2 31 88 11 76
The best patisserie in Trouville with cakes named after television personalities or literary figures. Just a couple of examples: the "Karl Zéro" Russian biscuit takes its name from a French television presenter; the macaroon with crème pâtissière whipped with white chocolate and raspberry, "Le Masque et la Plume" (The Mask and the Pen) is named for journalist and novelist Jérôme Garcin.

FERME DES AULNETTES
Route de la Corniche, 14510 Houlgate
Tel: + 33 (0)2 31 28 00 28
In this traditional inn with green shutters, the rustic-style dining room offers excellent local specialties

including free-range poultry, Norman camembert, and *sole meunière* with preserved tomatoes.

LA FEUILLE DE VIGNE

35, rue de la République, 14600 Honfleur
Tel: + 33 (0)2 31 89 22 35
One of the town's beautiful wine cellars, known for its nectars and sparkling ciders.

GRIBOUILLE

14, rue de l'Homme-des-Bois, 14600 Honfleur
Tel.: + 33 (0)2 31 89 29 54
Ciders and cider jelly, *pommeau* and *calvados* apple liqueurs, jams, biscuits, jars of tripe from Caen—these are only some of the exhaustive range of goods available in this unusual boutique. The tastiest of what the Norman terrain has to offer. (see photos pages 188–189)

LA PETITE CHINE

14-16, rue du Dauphin, 14600 Honfleur
Tel: + 33 (0)2 331 89 36 52
A patisserie and tearoom that also sells homemade cakes, caramels, and enticingly perfumed teas.

LES SABLES D'ASNELLES

17, rue Southampton, 14960 Asnelles
Tel: + 33 (0)2 31 22 32 09,
Fax: + 33 (0)2 3151 78 18
A patisserie in the heart of a village reputed for its delicious butter *sables* (shortbread cookies).

ARTISANS

APRES LA PLUIE

Kaléidoscope , Dominique Spora,
3, rue de la Libération
14950 Beaumont-en-Auge
Tel: + 33 (0)2 31 65 13 20

ATELIER CERAMIQUE TURGIS

Route de Saint-Lô, 14490 Noron la Poterie
Tel: + 33 (0)2 31 92 57 03
One of the workshops in a town that is a birthplace of Norman pottery.

BRIQUETERIE LAGRIVE

Glos – RN 13, 14100 Lisieux
A small brick factory that supplies materials for the upkeep of some of this area's facades.

MARTIAL MAYEL

Artisan glassmaker
27 rue du puits, 14600 Honfleur
Tel: + 33 (0)2 31 89 05 06
Fax: + 33 (0)2 31 89 42 46

Next to the house where Jongkind lived is the workshop of this master glassmaker who creates and restores magnificent stained-glass windows.

LA POTERIE DU MESNIL DE BAVENT

On the Caen-Cabourg road (D513)
14860 Bavent/Ranville
Tel: + 33 (0)2 31 84 82 41
www.poterie-bavent.com
A beautiful pottery workshop with an oak beam ceiling, that produces typically Norman terracotta wares. Guided visit of the workshop by appointment only. (see photos pages 192–193)

SMALL MUSEUMS

ABBAYE SAINT-MARTIN DE MONDAYE

14250 Mondaye
Tel: + 33 (0)2 31 92 58 11
This abbey with its own religious order is a magnificent jewel of the eighteenth century. Visits by guided tour only.

CHÂTEAU DE BALLEROY— MUSÉE DES BALLONS

Forbes Management Co. Inc.
B.P. 3, 14490 Balleroy
Tel, reception: + 33 (0)2 31 21 60 61
Tel, museum: + 33 (0)2 31 21 06 77
Built between 1626 and 1636 with local materials—gray stone and reddish flint—the château is one of the first works by François Mansart, who also created the church in the park. The residence later became a rally point for hot-air ballooners, whose feats provided a marvelous sight for spectators. Outside, the château is superb with gardens designed by Le Notre, and symmetrically-arranged buildings. The interior is equally impressive. Hunting scenes painted by Comte Albert de Balleroy, a nineteenth-century painter, decorate the salons on the ground floor; wooden objects in the dining room illustrate the fables of La Fontaine; the silk wall hangings in one of the bedrooms in the first floor are identical to those found in the Grand Trianon at the Château de Versailles.

CHÂTEAU DE FONTAINE HENRY

3, place du Château, 14610 Fontaine Henry
Tel: + 33 (0)2 31 80 00 42
Situated between Bayeux and Caen, this is a masterpiece of Renaissance architecture. The writer Jacques de Lacretelle described the residence as a "Loire valley château found in Normandy." Constructed by the Harcourt

family in the sixteenth century, the building has an intricate façade and displays paintings by Le Corrège, Mignard, Rigaud, and Hubert Robert in its pageantry rooms.

MUSÉE ALPHONSE ALLAIS

41 cours Albert Manuel, 14600 Honfleur
Tel: + 33 (0)2 31 89 74 38
The den of this nineteenth-century journalist and writer is striking for its shelves weighed down with poetically named magic potions, and above all, for its tiny dimensions. This was a former pharmacy that the assistant chemist and eccentric writer fitted out with a sense of humor. Demarais, one of the apothecaries who also worked here, created Passocéan, an elixir to ward off seasickness, and advertisements for this potion are still found on the exterior walls of the museum.

MUSÉE BARON GÉRARD

Rue Lambert Leforestier, 14400 Bayeux
Tel: + 33 (0)2 31 92 14 21
The museum displays porcelain and archaeology collections, as well as lace. The azure, ruby and gold perfume fountain and the Langlois tulip vases are only some of the items that take visitors on a lovely stroll through time.

MUSEE DU VIEUX HONFLEUR

Quai Saint-Étienne, 14600 Honfleur
Tel: + 33 (0)2 31 89 14 12
This museum brings together the extremes of water and land, the everyday and the infinite. The first part is dedicated to the sea and ship models. The building houses a church—an attempt to retrospectively bless the collections and those who live on the sea. The second part is more terrestrial, presenting items of regional furniture, everyday objects, seventeenth-century tiles from the Pays d'Auge, headdresses from previous centuries. A mixture of ethnography and popular art on show in twelve or so rooms, each dealing with a different theme.

MUSÉE EUGÈNE BOUDIN

Place Erik Satie, BP 80049, 14602 Honfleur
Tel: + 33 (0)2 31 89 54 00
A lovely collection of wardrobes, headdresses, engravings, costumes, and paintings illustrating life in Normandy in the eighteenth and nineteenth centuries.

MUSÉE LE VIEUX MANOIR

107, rue Grande, 14290 Orbec
Tel: + 33 (0)2 31 32 58 89
A strange timber-framed building, eccentric in

appearance with sculpted beams, brick walls, triangular stones, and stained-glass windows. Constructed in the sixteenth century, it now houses a municipal museum presenting the history of the area.

MUSÉE VIVANT DE LA BASSE-COUR

D 579, Norolles, 14100 Lisieux
Tel: + 33 (0)2 31 62 78 78
This one-of-a-kind private museum is home to nine hundred chickens, pigeons, ducks, geese, guinea-fowl and other birds that roam freely.

VILLA STRASSBURGER

Avenue Strassburger, 14800 Deauville
Tel: + 33 (0)2 31 88 20 44
One of the town's characteristic villas designed by architect G. Pichereau in the early 1900s. An archetype of the Belle Epoque style that is high on ornate details and the mixing of genres.

PARKS AND GARDENS

CHÂTEAU DE BRECY

14480 Saint-Gabriel-Brécy
Tel: + 33 (0)2 31 80 11 48
The region's most splendid terraced gardens, created in the eighteenth century and graced with Romantic sculptures. Praised in the works of writers Jean de la Varende and Jacques de Lacretelle. (see photos pages 68–69)

CHÂTEAU DE CANON

14270 Mezidon-Canon
Tel: + 33 (0)2 31 20 05 07
Advocate Jean-Baptiste-Elie de Beaumont, a friend of Voltaire, constructed this château in the eighteenth century, now classified as a historic monument. Only the park is open to the public. Its features include a pond, temples, Chinese pavilions, and *chartreuses* (small enclosures where fruit trees are grown). Enologist and sculptor in his spare time, Hervé de Mézerac recently opened a cellar in a dependency of the château, where regional products including delicious ciders and pear brandies are sold. (see photos pages 62–63)

CHTEAU D'HARCOURT

14220 Thury-Harcourt
Tel: + 33 (0)2 31 79 72 05
A magnificent garden with sage, perennials, hibiscuses, dahlias, petunias, and roses, right next to Caen.

CHÂTEAU DE VAULAVILLE
14400 Tour en Bessin
Tel: + 33 (0)2 31 92 52 62
A stunning eighteenth-century residence, classified as a historic monument.

JARDINS DES PAYS D'AUGE ET SES MAISONS A PANS DE BOIS
14340 Cambremer
Tel: + 33 (0)2 31 63 01 81
An estate right near Lisieux, with a garden filled with heady flowers, timber-framed houses, and a museum of antique tools that pays tribute to the area's arts and crafts. An entertaining and cultural outing.

JARDINS DE PLANT BESSIN
14490 Balleroy
Tel: + 33 (0)2 31 92 56 03
An alley of wisteria, a landscaped garden, a water garden, and above all, a collection of two thousand five hundred plants (some extremely rare) arranged according to seven themes, make up this garden between Bayeux and Saint-Lô. Special attention is paid to the geranium, a flower particularly cherished by the mistress of the garden and avid plant collector, Colette Sainte Beuve.

JARDIN DES PLANTES DE CAEN
5, place Blot, 14000 Caen
Tel: + 33 (0)2 31 30 48 30
A real lifeline of this town, with its orange grove, two greenhouses, and six thousand species of plants. In 1736, a botanical garden was added by a professor of medicine, Jean-Baptiste Caillard. Some years later, Francis Marescot, equally seduced by the magic of flowers, donated six hundred new plants to the site.

MANOIR DE BOUTEMONT
14100 Ouilly-le-Vicomte
Tel: + 33 (0)2 31 61 12 16
A pretty manor right near Lisieux, also worth visiting for the little tenth-century village church featuring a sixteenth-century lectern and a sculpted wooden altar. This garden à la Française, made up of a large pond, topiaries, and an Italian garden, won the title of "Remarkable Garden" in 2004. Visits by guided tour only, on Wednesdays and Saturdays at 3 P.M.

ANTIQUE DEALERS

JARDINS SECRETS
Secondhand items and furnishings
41 rue Mirabeau, 14800 Deauville
Tel: + 33 (0)2 31 87 35 57
An elegant selection of charming, refined objects and furniture is on display in this shop set up by an ex-Parisian right in the middle of Deauville. (see photo page 191)

CURIOSITIES

LA BELLE-ILOISE
6, rue des Logettes, 14600 Honfleur
Tel: + 33 (0)2 31 14 28 17
In a picturesque setting, this tinned-goods specialist sells the very best in tinned sardines, tuna, and peeled tomatoes.

"ART DECO" PHARMACY
78 rue du général De Gaulle
14440 Douvres la Délivrande
In the heart of the village and just next to the D-Day beaches, this establishment is conspicuous with its superb Belle Epoque façade. Inside, the elegant decor is enough to make one think that time has come to a standstill.

MANCHE

HOTELS

LA FOSSARDIERE
Hameau de la Fosse, 50440 Omonville-la-Petite
Tel: + 33 (0)2 33 52 19 83
A cluster of little houses, with blue stone or slate roofs, make up this streamside hamlet in a protected valley. Breakfast is served in the former bread oven. An ideal place to stop before visiting the house of poet Jacques Prévert or strolling on the heath of the Nez de Jobourg. (see photo page 163)

HOTEL LA BEAUMONDERIE
20, route de Coutances
50290 Breville-sur-mer
Tel: + 33 (0)2 33 50 36 36
Email: la-beaumonderie@wanadoo.fr
This superb 1900-style residence lodged General Eisenhower in 1944. Its dining room has a veranda looking over the garden, and all the rooms offer an unbeatable view of the Chausey, Jersey, and Guernsey Islands. Service is warm and the setting extremely elegant.

HOTEL NEPTUNE
Promenoir Jersey, 50230 Agon-Coutainville
Tel: + 33 (0)2 33 47 07 66
A little hotel, white from top to bottom, skillfully managed by a team of young owners. Right at the water's edge, the hotel offers eleven rooms (numbers two and nine have three windows overlooking the sea), a bar, a terrace with several tables from which to contemplate the ocean, common rooms with pretty fittings, and a book-filled library for days when the weather is temperamental. Parisians cherish this little resort town where long strolls up to the lighthouse of Agon at sunset are not to be missed. Here, the sea and the sand change color every hour of the day. (see photo page 163)

LE MASCARET
Ancien presbytère
16, rue Sienne
50200 Heugueville sur Seine
Tel: + 33 (0)2 33 45 86 09
No accommodation is available in the former presbytery itself, but the owners offer bed-and-breakfast rooms nearby. Homegrown products feature in the restaurant.

BED-AND-BREAKFASTS

CHÂTEAU DE BOUCEEL
50240 Vergoncey
Tel: + 33 (0)2 33 48 34 61
Email: chateaudebouceel@wanadoo.fr
The Count and Countess Régis de Roquefeuil-Cahuzac are owners of this residence that boasts a delicious old-world flavor.

CHÂTEAU DE COIGNY
50250 Coigny
Tel: + 33 (0)2 33 42 10 79
Email: coigny@free.fr
Odette Ionckheere
Not far from Carentan sits this charming residence in the middle of the countryside. Far from the main roads, it is thus idyllically calm. Property owner Odette Ionckheere offers two bedrooms, the first Louis XIII, the second Louis XVI.

CHÂTEAU DE L'ISLE MARIE
50360 Picauville
Tel: + 33 (0)2 33 21 37 25
Email: dorothea@islemarie.com
Dorothée de la Houssaye and Simon Rock de Besombes have made their residence into a fairy-tale castle. Situated at the end of a tree-lined alley, the château disposes of five comfortable guest rooms with canopy beds, a living room, a dining room and a book-lined library. In the park, a little manor house is divided into two apartments, each containing a kitchen, for family holidays. (see photo page 167)

FERME-MANOIR LA FEVRERIE
10, route d'Arville, 50760 Sainte-Geneviève
Tel: + 33 (0)2 33 54 33 53
A manor built in the sixteenth century, fitted out with luxurious furniture and inviting fabrics. Breakfast is served on the beautiful wooden table in the dining room, near the fireplace.

LE FORT DU CAP LEVI
50840 Fermanville
Tel: + 33 (0)2 33 23 68 68
Email: chambre_fermanville@cq50.fr
An original and enchanting seaside experience in the heart of a Napoleonic fort, perched on pink granite rocks. With their bright blue or red quilts, the rooms are comfortably equipped and the welcome very friendly. The mornings here are particularly delightful thanks to breakfasts with an unforgettable view. Our favorite spot on this coast. (see photo page 163)

MANOIR DU VAL JOUET
50260 Le Vretot
Tel: + 33 (0)2 33 52 24 42
A small, stone manor, hidden away from the main roads, between Bricquebec and Carteret. The garden is so pretty and the welcome so pleasant that it is necessary to book well in advance to get a room.

RESTAURANTS AND BISTROS

L'AUBERGE DE GOURY
50440 Auderville
Tel: + 33 (0)2 33 52 77 01
Highly hospitable. Here, tables are arranged around a fireplace where fish and meat cook over embers, while the windows overlook the Baie de Goury and its lighthouse. This is the place to go for magnificent scenery—a pleasant place to stop after a spectacular hike on the Chemin des Douaniers, or after a stroll from one cape to another to admire this wild coast where several granite villages are lodged. (see photo page 179)

LE CHASSE-MAREE
8, place du Général de Gaulle
50550 Saint-Vaast-la-Hougue
Tel: + 33 (0)2 33 23 14 08
Found on the port, this simple yet refined restaurant decked out in yacht club décor serves delicious seafood.

LES GRANDES MARQUES

La Place, 50330 Saint-Pierre-Eglise
Tel: + 33 (0)2 33 43 08 11

This brasserie looks out onto the town's central square. The old-fashioned façade and décor of this long-standing bistro provide a friendly pub atmosphere where the service is always warm. (see photo page 178)

RESTAURANT
LE MOULIN A VENTS

Hameau Danneville (Danneville hamlet)
50440 Saint-Germain-des-Vaux
Tel: + 33 (0)2 33 52 75 20

In a natural setting not far from the smallest port in France, Port Racine, this restaurant offers delicious meals based on whatever fresh products are available. Moreover, in summer its open terrace offers a stunning view of the sea.

RESTAURANT LE SEMAPHORE

La vigie Semaphore, 50340 Flamanville
Tel: + 33 (0)2 33 52 18 98

A breathtaking location, right on the sea. After a stroll in the exquisite park of the Château de Flamanville, don't miss out on trying the Sémaphore crêpes. (Phone to find out the opening dates).

GOURMET STORES

GOSSELIN

Fine foods store
27, rue de Verrue, 50550 Saint-Vaast-la-Hougue
Tel: + 33 (0)2 33 54 40 06

This famous traditional store is known for its exhaustive selection of high-quality fine foods, including the best regional products. (see photo page 187)

HUITRERIE DE SAINT-VAAST

Société Hélie & Fils, 47, rue d'Isamberville
50550 Saint-Vaast-La-Houghe
Tel: + 33 (0)2 33 54 42 70

Here, the seabed slopes gently and the oysters are rocked by the best currents in Europe. The natural setting produces seafood with a distinct flavor. The oyster farm stretches out over more than 75 acres (30 ha) and the oysters—the best in the region—are sold to members of the public.

LA MAISON DU BISCUIT

Place Costard, 50270 Sortosville-en-Beaumont
Tel: + 33 (0)2 33 04 09 04

This traditional biscuit shop found on the road between Bricquebec and Barneville in the Cotentin is an absolute must. Many are the customers who come to buy biscuits and fine foods from this place that bears a distinct likeness to Ali Baba's cavern. The shop was created by a cunning decorator to resemble an old-fashioned boutique with an adjoining tearoom. The biscuits here are in a class of their own. Every day, fine, fragile almond *tuiles* or delectable *financiers* emerge fresh from the ovens. From Wednesday to Saturday, you can find chunky Savoie cookies and on Sunday morning the renowned brioche is available. Marc Burnouf, creator of these exquisite delicacies, will be happy to tell you the beautiful story of the family who manages this boutique. (see photo page 185)

LA MERE POULARD

Grand Rue – BP 18,
50116 Le Mont-Saint-Michel
Tel: + 33 (0)2 33 89 68 68

The famous boutique of the legendary inn and restaurant on Mont-Saint-Michel, very popular for its elegant room with a stone fireplace and above all for its famous runny omelettes cooked in copper pots.

ARTISANS

LA BOUTIQUE DU CHÂTEAU

Cabinetmaking
Ebenisterie, Claude Brosselin
Château de Hemevez, 50700 Valognes
Tel: + 33 (0)2 33 21 33 02

Claude Brosselin designs and produces furniture inspired from the styles of yesteryear and adapted to modern-day life. Oak furniture waxed and polished, varnished inlaid furniture, hand-painted beech-wood furniture … the collection is made up of large furniture items—shelves and tables—that can be made to measure according to specified dimensions and preferred colors.

MAITRE POTIER DE BARFLEUR

Patrick Lefebvre
56, rue Saint Nicolas, 50760 Barfleur
Tel: + 33 (0)2 33 23 11 51

The pottery and ceramic workshop of Patrick Lefebvre displays stunning one-off pieces: vases, dishes, and jugs in various tones of blue or brown. The creator also makes finials and colored ridge tiles that he calls "taffettes."

SMALL MUSEUMS

MAISON DE BARBEY D'AUREVILLY

66, rue Bottin-Desylles
50390 Saint-Sauveur-le-Vicomte
Tel: + 33 (0)2 33 41 65 18

Found in the town of birth of the nineteenth-century writer, this little museum holding a bust of Barbey d'Aurevilly by renowned sculptor Auguste Rodin, will certainly be appreciated by those with a passion for his work. The village is not particularly interesting, but readers who manage to recognize landscapes described in his books, notably in Carteret or Valognes (for example the exquisite Hôtel de Beaumont or the Château de l'Isle Marie called "Château des Saules" in his writings), will no doubt be able to satisfy their curiosity here.

MAISON DE JACQUES PREVERT

Le Val, 50440 Omonville la Petite
Tel: + 33 (0)2 33 52 72 38

It is in this stone house with the pretty garden that the poet lived for seventeen years—the last years of a very studious life, for he never left the first floor that he turned into a huge work studio. Prévert was persuaded to live in this minuscule village where even today there is no bistro, by the famous cinema set decorator Alexandre Trauner. The two are buried side by side in the village cemetery overlooking the sea, their simple stone tombs now covered by vegetation. (see photo page 97)

MAISON
DE JEAN-FRANÇOIS MILLET

Hameau-Gruchy, 50440 Gréville-Hague
Tel: + 33 (0)2 33 04 26 69

The point of Cotentin and the nearby Hague are some of the landscapes that inspired artist Jean-François Millet. Now open to the public, the house where Millet was born in the hamlet of Gruchy, near Grèville, was the theme in a number of his works. Paintings depicting all landscapes of the region and all aspects of rural life of the time can be found in the Boston Art Museum, which holds the largest collection of Millet's works, before Japanese, then French galleries. The museum visit finishes in a room exhibiting effigies of *The Gleaners* and *The Angelus*. (see photo pages 194–195)

PARKS AND GARDENS

CHÂTEAU AND PARC
DE NACQUEVILLE

50460 Urville-Nacqueville
Tel: + 33 (0)2 33 03 21 12

A romantic park conceived by an English landscape designer for Hippolyte de Tocqueville (the brother of the prominent nineteenth-century politician Alexis who lived in the neighboring château and who wrote: "My brother has made this place into one of the prettiest places on earth"). The park is the perfect setting for the château, before which stands a stone barrier with a draw gate. Towards the sea, the grounds feature a stream, waterfalls cutting through flowery slopes, and a long lawn. The park is particularly spectacular in June, when the rhododendrons in bloom cover the undergrowth with a purple carpet. (see photo page 78)

JARDIN BOTANIQUE
DU CHÂTEAU DE VAUVILLE

50440 Beaumont-Hague
Tel: + 33 (0)2 33 10 00 00
Fax: + 33 (0)2 33 10 00 01

Perhaps you will have the good fortune of being guided through this park by Cléophée de Turkheim. It is she and her husband who live in the Château de Vauville and who run this garden dedicated to plants from the southern hemisphere. However, if the lady of the manor is not around, you will be shown through the palm trees, eucalyptuses, and gunneras by others equally passionate about these plants. The striking garden changes in appearance from month to month. Close to the ponds not far from the sea, a cafeteria and picnic tables have recently been installed, allowing you to take a break in one of the most astonishing landscapes of the Cotentin. You can also buy plants for your own garden here. By all means take the spectacular Route de la Hay de Tôt to get here—this coastal itinerary offers a spectacular view of the water and greenery that have made the area into a bird haven. (see photo page 83)

JARDIN EN HOMMAGE
A JACQUES PREVERT

Vallée des Moulins
50440 Saint-Germain-des-Vaux

No telephone number available for this very secret garden open in the afternoon from Easter to October (closed Fridays). Its creator Gérard Fusberti was close to Prévert. Along with others who knew the poet, he came up with an original idea for a way to pay homage to their common friend two years after his death: the creation of a waterside garden featuring waterfalls, abandoned windmills, and a tree planted by each friend. Around the spectacular gunnera hedges, visitors will discover the pine trees of singer and actor Yves Montand, the lime-blossom tree of photographer Robert Doisneau, the eucalyptus of singer Mouloudji, or the pink birches of Oona Chaplin, wife of the famous Charlie. You can stop at little benches and baroque bridges along your stroll through this enchanting place. In 2004, the garden came first in a competition for the most beautiful private garden.

MUSEE AND JARDIN CHRISTIAN DIOR

Les Rhumbs, 50400 Granville
Tel: + 33 (0)2 33 61 48 21
Les Rhumbs, the pink villa bought by the parents of *haute couture* designer Christian Dior at the start of the last century, now houses a fashion museum whose cliff-side garden overlooks the ocean. All this is found at the end of the seaside Promenade du Plat-Gousset. In the museum, all of the fashion collections have been put together thanks to donations and acquisitions. As well as pieces produced by the prestigious fashion house, the museum displays drawings by Dior and also by his collaborators such as Gruau and Blossac. Every year, a new exhibition is organized. (see photo page 88–89)

PARC DE BEAUREPAIRE

Château de Martinvast, 50690 Martinvast
Tel: + 33 (0)2 33 87 20 80
Around the château built in the sixteenth century and renovated in the nineteenth century, is a park covering 250 acres (100 ha). A fine example of the wonders of recycling, for the marsh surrounding the domain was transformed into a circuit made up of a pond, waterfalls, and forests. The park's creator and former owner Baron Schickler was responsible for the exotic tone of this coastal domain that features conifers, cypresses, plane trees, American oaks, tulips, sequoias, rhododendrons, and even palm trees.

ANTIQUE DEALERS

MONTEBOURG ANTIQUITES

38, rue du Général Leclerc, Montebourg
Tel: + 33 (0)2 33 41 24 85
A very good antique shop in this region where antique wares are not so easy to find.

Jacques Legebre displays furniture and art objects from the eighteenth and nineteenth centuries.

CHÂTEAUX

CHÂTEAU DE CROSVILLE-SUR-DOUVE

Crosville-sur-Douve, 50360 Picanville
Tel: + 33 (0)2 33 41 67 25
Michèle Lefol is a dynamic young woman who has worked with a passion to restore this château that is well worth visiting for its sumptuous pageantry room. Numerous gatherings and exhibitions are organized here, especially during the evening in summer when garden produce is served at receptions. Michèle Lefol reveals her cooking secrets in an attractive book, *Recettes secrètes des jardiniers de Normandie*. In April, an annual Franco-British plant festival is held. (see photo pages 116–117).

Bibliography

Discovering the region

Beautheac, Nadine. *La Normandie de Proust*. Editions du Chêne, 2001.

Caracola, Jean-Paul & Biollay, Gustave. *Normandy*. Rizzoli, 1992.

Dannenberg, Linda, Levec, Pierre & Levin, Pierre. *Pierre Deux's Normandy: A French Country Style and Sourcebook*. Clarkson N. Potter, 1998.

Decoin, Didier. *Cherbourg, La Hague* (essays). 1991.

Decoin, Didier (text) & Courault, Patrick (photographs). *Presqu'île de lumière, rivages du Cotentin*. Isoète, 1996.

Delerm, Philippe. *Rouen*. PUF, 1987.

Delerm, Philippe & Martine (photographs). *Les Chemins nous inventent*. Livre de Poche, 1999.

Fauchon, Regis & Lescroart, Yves. *Manor Houses in Normandy*. Konemann, 1999.

Gaudez, René & Champollion, Hervé. *Promenade en Normandie*. Ouest France, 1996.

Granville, Patrick (text) & Pelletier-Lattes, Micheline (photographs). *Au long des haies de Normandie*. Edition du Chêne, 1980.

Home, Gordon. *Normandy: The Scenery and Romance of its Ancient Towns*. Kessinger Publishing, 2004.

Lenclos, Jean Philippe & Dominique. *Les Couleurs de la France*. Editions du Moniteur, 2003.

Loomis, Susan. *On Rue Tatin: Living and Cooking in a Small French Town*. Broadway Books, 2001.

Palmer, Hugh. *The Most Beautiful Villages of Normandy*. Thames and Hudson, 2002.

Pontavice, Gilles & Bleuzen de. *La Cuisine des châteaux de Normandie*. Editions Ouest France, 1998.

Revert, Jacques (text) & Braque, Georges (paintings). *Varengeville*. Maeght, 1968.

Robert, Herbert. *Monet on the Normandy Coast: Tourism and Painting: 1867–1886*. Yale University Press, 1994.

Satiat, Nadine. *Maupassant*. Flammarion, 2003.

Silverstone, Rob. *A Mule in Rouen: A Discovery of Upper Normandy*. Vanguard Press, 2004.

Smith, Judy. *Holiday Walks in Normandy*. Sigma Press, 2001.

Valery, Marie-Françoise (text), Motte, Vincent (photographs) & Sarramon, Christian (photographs). *Gardens in Normandy*. Flammarion, 1995.

Verger, François-Xavier. *La Route des Abbayes normandes*. Editions du Huitième Jour, 2003.

Warrell, Ian. *Turner on the Seine*. Tate Gallery Publications, 1999.

Guidebooks

Bienvenue au château. Association Bienvenue au château, France de l'Ouest, Nantes.
Calvados. Guides Gallimard.
DK Eyewitness Top 10 Travel Guides Normandy. DK Publishing.
Eure. Guides Gallimard.
Gîtes au jardin 2004. Maison et Gîtes de France et du Tourisme vert, 59 rue Saint-Lazare, 75009 Paris.
Insight Guide Normandy. Langenscheidt Publishing Co.
Manche. Guides Gallimard.
Normandy and the Seine. French Ramblers Association. McCarta Publishing, 1991.
Normandy Cotentin Green Guide. Michelin Travel Publications.
Normandy Green Guide. Michelin Travel Publications.
Normandy Seine Valley Green Guide. Michelin Travel Publications.
Seine-Maritime. Guides Gallimard.

Index

Index of place names

Index of proper names

Acknowledgments

The editor is grateful to the following individuals for their warm welcome in Normandy and their excellent advice that was invaluable in creating this book:
Madame Achard, Paula Almquist, José Alvarez, Thierry and Béatrice Ardisson, Béatrice Augié, Arlette and François Barré, Antoine Bouchayer-Mallet, Pierre Brinon, Jérôme Darblay, Didier and Chantal Decoin, Philippe Delerm, Frank Ferrand, Isabelle and Marc Guinoiseau, Antoine and Chantal Hébrard, Dorothée de la Houssaye, Jean Lou Janeir, Jennifer Jean, Philippe Landry, Nicole Legrand, Yves Lescroart, Susan Loomis, Frédéric Morel, Marie-Pierre Morel, Côme Mosta-Heirst, Pascal Retout, Cléophée de Turckheim.

The author would like to thank in particular:
Inès, Morvane, Elisabeth Bailliée, Marc Burnouf, Jean de Castilla, Anita Coppet, Véronique de Coppet, Ysabel and René Courcelle, Laurence and Alban Cristin, Jérôme Darblay, Jean-Jacques Driewir, Godeleine and Philippe Legrix de la Salle, Anne-Marie Mesnil, Marie-Pierre Morel, Philippe Séguret, Jean Claude Roucheray, Cléophée de Turckheim, and all those who generously opened their doors and unveiled their treasures.

Heartfelt thanks go to Loréa Albistur and Felicity Bodenstein for their help throughout the compilation of this work.

All photos in this book were taken by Christian Sarramon with the exception of the photograph on page 149: © Jérôme Darblay.

Translated from the French by Susan Pickford, Sheila O'Leary, and Fui Lee Luk
Copyediting: Jennifer Ladonne
Typesetting: Barbara Kekus
Proofreading: Slade Smith
Color Separation: Penez Éditions
Maps: Edigraphie

Distributed in North America by Rizzoli International Publications.

Previously published in French as
L'Art de Vivre en Normandie
© Éditions Flammarion, 2004

English-language edition
© Éditions Flammarion, 2005

05 06 07 4 3 2 1
FC0477-05-III
ISBN: 2-0803-0477-1
Dépôt légal: 03/2005

Printed in Italy by Canle